The Unequal Effects of Globalization

The Ohlin Lectures
David Domeij, series editor

See http://mitpress.mit.edu for a complete list of titles in this series.

The Unequal Effects of Globalization

Pinelopi Koujianou Goldberg

with Greg Larson

The MIT Press
Cambridge, Massachusetts
London, England

Support for this project was provided by the Economic Growth Center at Yale University.

Yale *Economic Growth Center*

The MIT Press would like to thank the anonymous peer reviewers who provided comments on drafts of this book. The generous work of academic experts is essential for establishing the authority and quality of our publications. We acknowledge with gratitude the contributions of these otherwise uncredited readers.

This book was set in Palatino LT Std by New Best-set Typesetters Ltd. Printed and bound in the United States of America.

Library of Congress Cataloging-in-Publication Data

Names: Goldberg, Pinelopi K., author. | Larson, Gregory M., author.
Title: The unequal effects of globalization / Pinelopi Koujianou
  Goldberg ; with Greg Larson.
Description: Cambridge, Massachusetts : The MIT Press, [2023] |
  Series: Ohlin lectures | Includes bibliographical references and index.
Identifiers: LCCN 2022046852 (print) | LCCN 2022046853 (ebook) |
  ISBN 9780262048255 (hardcover) | ISBN 9780262375573 (epub) |
  ISBN 9780262375566 (pdf)
Subjects: LCSH: International economic integration—History. |
  Globalization—Economic aspects. | Globalization—Economic
  aspects—Developing countries. | Developing countries—Foreign
  economic relations. | Equality—Developing countries.
Classification: LCC HF1418.5 .G6445 2023 (print) |
  LCC HF1418.5 (ebook) | DDC 337—dc23/eng/20221121
LC record available at https://lccn.loc.gov/2022046852
LC ebook record available at https://lccn.loc.gov/2022046853

Contents

Preface

Globalization is currently a central focus of concern and debate among academics, policy makers, and—increasingly—the general public. Of course, the phenomenon of globalization is nothing new. Since the ancient Sumerian and Greek civilizations, long-distance trade in goods has been a source of wealth for nations, while broader forms of globalization, from migration and exploration to cultural cross-fertilization, have always been an essential feature of humankind. What is new, however, is the dramatic change in the scope and speed of globalization from the late 1990s until the financial crisis of 2008—a period labeled as the "age of hyperglobalization"—and the more recent trends against it.

At a critical moment of shifting attitudes, policies, and politics related to globalization, this monograph enters the debate while also taking a step back in order to assess the recent evolution of global trade, and its unequal effects between and within countries. The sections that follow will investigate globalization's many dimensions, disruptions, and complex interactions, from the late twentieth century's wave of trade liberalizations to the rise of China, decline of manufacturing in advanced economies, and recent effects of trade on global poverty, inequality, labor markets, and firm dynamics. The monograph will explore the significance of the recent backlash against and retreat from globalization as well.

Structurally, the monograph is organized into three main sections. The first section examines the key features of the recent period of hyperglobalization (and the post–World War II "age of globalization" that preceded it) as well as offers an overview of the emerging retreat. The second section argues that two factors likely contributed to this retreat: the perceptions that global trade and international competition have not been fair, and that this lack of fairness has also exacerbated inequality within countries. The third and final section briefly considers the key policy implications of these trends and emerging dynamics; in particular, it emphasizes—amid the possibility of an emerging era of deglobalization—the potential of place-based policies as well as the critical importance of international cooperation.

The monograph is based on my Ohlin lecture at the Stockholm School of Economics on November 4, 2019. As such, its goal is to provide a succinct overview of the effects that globalization may have had on inequality. It does not claim that globalization was the sole or even most significant factor driving inequality; clearly, many other concurrent developments (such as technology and automation in particular) played an important role. Moreover, the monograph does not attempt an in-depth analysis of inequality and its drivers, nor does it offer a horse race between the many alternative hypotheses as to which factors are responsible for the perceived increase in inequality in recent years. A major, multiyear research project is currently in the works at the Institute of Fiscal Studies to provide such a comprehensive analysis—Inequality: The Deaton Review, led by an interdisciplinary panel of which I am a member. Several relevant findings from the Deaton

Review are highlighted in this monograph, but I encourage interested readers to visit the project's website to explore its broader preliminary results.[1] The themes covered in the project—from the history, geography, and political economy of inequality to its manifestations across several domains, including gender, race and ethnicity, health, early child development, education, immigration, firms, the labor market, and globalization, as well as the dynamics around policy responses like redistribution and the benefits system—reveal the complex, multidimensional nature of the inequality phenomenon.

The monograph also focuses narrowly on the trade dimensions of globalization rather than on some of its broader aspects, such as migration. Like trade, any given country's approach to migration typifies its global orientation and the relative openness of its borders. Migration's effects on economic growth and inequality—real or imagined in the public sphere—have played an important role in the recent backlash against globalization. But migration and trade are fundamentally separate issues: goods on the move are different from people on the move, and immigration raises complex issues that trade typically does not—including national identity and culture, which are highly salient in many countries' debates over immigration, particularly in Europe and the United States. The economic and policy implications of migration and trade are also quite distinct. There is clear evidence in the economics literature that immigration (notwithstanding some significant exceptions) is typically beneficial for both migrants and receiving countries. This is especially true in countries with labor shortages due to shifting demographic trends, like many European countries. While the effects of migration on source countries are somewhat less well understood, it is apparent that the emigration of skilled workers can lead to "brain drain" in these countries—or more generally, "ability drain," given that many unskilled migrants are still highly motivated individuals with enormous potential for entrepreneurship and productivity. (This is an area where I have some personal experience as a native of Greece who has spent most of my career in the United States; I would like to think that the immigration of people like myself is generally good for the receiving country, though the long-run effects of mass emigration on the countries we leave behind are less clear.) These are crucial and relevant issues for the economic and policy debates about globalization—but for the purposes of this monograph, I will focus squarely on trade.

Likewise, the monograph does not focus on all the ancillary features of globalization, such as capital mobility. Recent decades have seen enormous growth in global capital flows as well as significant policy changes that have removed or loosened capital controls and liberalized exchange rate regimes in many countries around the world. Such enhanced capital mobility has fostered trade growth, foreign direct investment, and the formation of global value chains, serving as an integral aspect of the hyperglobalization in the 1990s and 2000s. This era of essentially unfettered capital mobility has many implications that this monograph explores, such as the rise of large multinational "superstar" firms and the question of how capital should be taxed in light of globalization's unequal effects. The broad features, drivers, and effects of capital mobility, however, fall outside the scope of this monograph's look at one particular aspect of globalization: the relationship between international trade and inequality.[2]

At the time of the Ohlin lecture, I was the chief economist of the World Bank Group. The views expressed in the lecture and this monograph are my own and do not represent those of the World Bank. Since the end of 2019, the world has changed dramatically, and the COVID-19 pandemic has had profound effects on both globalization and inequality. The data underlying this monograph predate the pandemic, and I will not attempt any speculation regarding the long-run effects of the global health and economic crises on the nature of globalization and inequality; it is too early for such an undertaking. Nevertheless, I will occasionally qualify statements referring to the pre-COVID era, pointing to trends that have recently emerged in response to the pandemic.

Acknowledgments

I thank the Stockholm School of Economics, especially my host David Domeij, for inviting me to deliver the 2019 Ohlin lecture on which this monograph is based. Likewise, thanks to the MIT Press, particularly Emily Taber, for inviting me to turn that lecture into a book for the Ohlin Lectures series, and the two reviewers who provided many constructive comments. I am grateful to Yale's Economic Growth Center—especially Rohini Pande, Deanna Ford, and Vestal McIntyre—for supporting the drafting of the manuscript. Greg Larson offered invaluable writing support, and Rada Pavlova expertly reproduced and designed the monograph's figures. The Ohlin lecture and this monograph draw heavily on my past and current work, much of which has been undertaken with many esteemed colleagues from Yale and other institutions—including the 2020 *World Development Report* team during my time as the chief economist of the World Bank. I am immensely grateful to them all. Thanks especially to Jan De Loecker, Amit Khandelwal, Nina Pavcnik, Michele Ruta, Max Schwarz, and Daria Taglioni for helping update the data, figures, and analysis included in this monograph.

1 The Age of (Hyper)Globalization

1.1 General Trends

Until recently, the prevailing economic consensus was that humanity was living through an unprecedented "age of globalization": a period defined by increasing global connections through commerce and trade amid continual technological progress and a sustained period of broad geopolitical stability. But what does the "age of globalization" really mean in terms of its economic aspects—and what does it mean, moreover, that we may be living through its end?

In terms of an economic definition of the "age of globalization," two defining features stand out. First, over the course of several decades after World War II, all *measurable* trade barriers—by which we principally mean tariff levels—declined dramatically. While there are also, of course, important nontariff trade barriers (e.g., quantitative restrictions on imports, such as quotas, or the "voluntary" export restraints applied to the US automobile industry in the early 1980s), they are harder to measure, and it is not clear that they have decreased to the same extent, as discussed below. Figure 1.1 shows the average US tariff levels between 1875 and 2019: while more or less

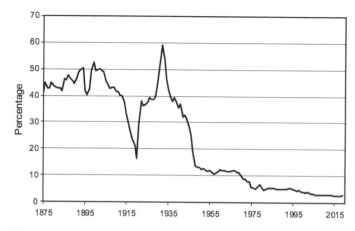

Figure 1.1
Average US tariffs, 1875–2019. *Sources:* World Development Indicators, "Tariff Rate, Applied, Simple Mean, Manufactured Products (%)—United States" (Washington, DC: World Bank Group, n.d.); US Bureau of the Census, "Historical Statistics of the United States: Colonial Times to 1970" (Washington, DC: US Department of Commerce, 1975); US Bureau of the Census, "1970–1988, Highlights of US Export and Import Trade, Series FT 990, Monthly; Beginning 1989, US Merchandise Trade: Selected Highlights, Series FT 920," Washington, DC: US Department of Commerce, n.d.).

stable in the late nineteenth and early twentieth centuries (notwithstanding a temporary reduction during World War I and temporary spike during the interwar years), US tariffs declined sharply after World War II. From 1975 to 2019 (not including the outlier year of 1979), the average US tariff was less than 6 percent. This trend was not limited to the United States, and recent decades have seen an acceleration in the decline of tariffs around the globe to levels that are very low by historical standards. These trends also coincided with a sharp, technology-driven decline in transportation and communication costs, as discussed later in this section; together, the decline in policy-driven tariff

Figure 1.2
The age of globalization: World exports as percentage of GDP, 1827–2019.
Source: Data from 1827 to 2014 from Michel Fouquin and Jules Hugot, "Two Centuries of Bilateral Trade and Gravity Data: 1827–2014" (CEPII Working Paper No. 2016–14, May 2016), http://www.cepii.fr/pdf_pub/wp/2016/wp2016-14.pdf. Data from 2015 to 2019 extends Fouquin and Hugot, "Two Centuries of Bilateral Trade and Gravity Data," using the author's estimates derived from World Bank, "Exports of Goods and Services (% of GDP)," World Bank Group, accessed July 25, 2022, https://data.worldbank.org/indicator/NE.EXP.GNFS.ZS.

barriers and developments in technology resulted in a pronounced decline of trade costs.

Such historically low trade costs enabled the other key feature of the "age of globalization": an explosion of global trade volumes in the post–World War II period. Figure 1.2 shows how world exports, fairly constant in the nineteenth and early twentieth centuries, began rising after World War II and accelerated dramatically in the late 1990s and early 2000s—a period now known as hyperglobalization that coincided with the emergence of global value chains (GVCs). The export share of global GDP peaked in 2007, before the global financial crisis. After dropping sharply during 2007 and 2008, global exports quickly bounced back, but they have not yet recovered to precrisis levels. In the late 2010s, the growth of exports slowed—a trend we will explore more in later sections. The graph stops in 2019, before the onset of the global COVID-19 pandemic. While the pandemic and the economic crisis that followed did of course impact trade, globalization, and inequality, it is still too early to assess its complex long-term effects and interactions. As discussed in the preface, for the purposes of this monograph, we consider the unequal effects of globalization up to the pandemic's onset in early 2020.

Importantly, the fast rise of trade in the post–World War II period was not driven by a single country or group of countries. While certain large developing countries— China, for instance—experienced particularly rapid export growth, many other developing countries also became integrated into the world trading system during this period. Figure 1.3 compares the global trend from the previous

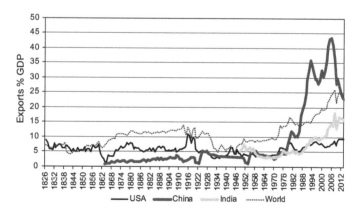

Figure 1.3
The age of globalization: Exports as percentage of GDP, 1827–2014. *Source:* Michel Fouquin and Jules Hugot, "Two Centuries of Bilateral Trade and Gravity Data: 1827–2014" (CEPII Working Paper No. 2016–14, May 2016), http://www.cepii.fr/pdf_pub/wp/2016/wp2016-14.pdf.

figure against the experiences of China, India, the United States, and the rest of the world.[1] Clearly, Chinese market reforms in the late 1970s led to a sharp increase in China's exports-to-GDP ratio, which rose from 4 percent in 1977 to 41 percent in 2007. While this increase did have a large effect on the global trend, simply due to the size of China's economy, other countries also contributed. India's export share, for instance, increased from 5 to 14 percent over the same three decades. Certainly, advanced economies were not a major driver of the global trend; the US export share increased only modestly during the postwar period, from 4 percent in 1945 to 9 percent in 2014.

The important role of developing countries in the "age of globalization"—low-income countries, in particular—is strikingly illustrated by figure 1.4.[2] Between 1985 and 2015, the composition of world exports changed dramatically in terms of country income groups. In 1985, exports from high-income countries accounted for about 87 percent of world trade. But over the next thirty years, the combined share of the other three groups—upper-middle-income, lower-middle-income, and low-income countries—increased from about 13 percent to about 32 percent of world trade. (Note that country income groups are expressed here in time-invariant categories based on the World Bank's 1987 classifications.)

Low-income countries experienced the largest growth of any income group during this period, increasing from 2.8 to 16.7 percent of world trade. Again, China is a major driver of these shifts—categorized in figure 1.4 as a low-income country (as it was in 1987) despite graduating to lower-middle-income status in the late 1990s and upper-middle-income status a decade later. The global integration of many other developing countries, however, also played an important role; lower-middle-income countries,

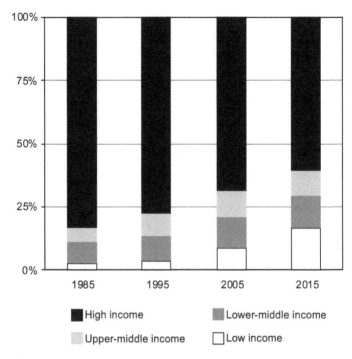

Figure 1.4
Composition of world exports by income group. *Source:* Nina Pavcnik,
"The Impact of Trade on Inequality in Developing Countries," *Jackson
Hole Economic Policy Symposium Proceedings* (Kansas City: Federal Reserve
Bank of Kansas City, August 2017), 67.

for example, increased their share of world trade from
8.5 to 12.6 percent. The increasing importance of developing countries in world trade reflects their participation in
GVCs, as we explore at length throughout the monograph.

1.2   The Persistent (and Underrated) Importance of Trade Policy

What were the underlying drivers of this long era of trade
growth? Economists have been debating this question for

decades. While falling tariff levels during the postwar period were a major factor, a new consensus has emerged in recent years—shared by academics and policy makers alike—that the explosion of global trade volumes in the late twentieth century cannot be explained by trade policy. This view holds that more important factors were at play, namely technology, and that globalization was both inevitable and unstoppable. According to this new consensus, technological developments in the late twentieth century made the world ever more connected, while also leading to a steady decline in the costs of transportation and communication, which together allowed global trade to flourish. By extension, this view holds that trade policy—that is, the imposition and reduction of tariffs as well as the signing of trade agreements, first within General Agreement on Tariffs and Trade (GATT) and then within the World Trade Organization (WTO)—was more or less irrelevant to global trade levels by the end of the twentieth century.[3]

This view is reflected in several recent quotes from the popular press. For example, in an article on the benefits and perceived risks of the proposed Trans-Pacific Partnership (TPP), the *New York Times* noted in 2015,

[One myth undermining support for the TPP] is that recent trade agreements have hurt jobs. . . . This argument fails to differentiate between the impacts of increased global trade and those of trade agreements. [It] is globalization, technology, and flawed educational and tax systems that are driving this trend, *not trade pacts*.[4]

One might think that this view is only held by journalists who are not familiar with the specifics of trade policy. Indeed, as economist Paul Krugman wrote in 1995,

Most journalistic discussion of the growth of world trade seems to view growing integration as driven by a technological imperative—to believe that improvements in transportation and communication technology constitute an irresistible force dissolving national boundaries. International economists, however, tend to view much, though not all, of the growth of trade as having essentially political causes, seeing its great expansion after World War II largely as a result of the removal of the protectionist measures that had constricted world markets since 1913.[5]

More than two decades after Krugman made this statement, however, the view that trade policy plays only a secondary role in the growing importance of international trade is no longer confined to journalistic circles; it has now become dominant in academic research. The new consensus is reflected in this 2008 quote from economist Lant Pritchett: "Relative to when I started working as a trade economist in the early 1980s, the world is completely liberalized. . . . [T]he incremental gains from anything that could happen as a result of WTO negotiations are just infinitesimal."[6]

While Pritchett does not explicitly claim that trade policy and trade agreements are irrelevant, he suggests that despite their significant effects in the past, their own success has rendered them irrelevant, and any incremental gains from further liberalization are destined to be small. Many academic economists would agree with this statement, and some would go even further, claiming that trade policy never had significant effects; indeed, they could invoke a considerable body of work to support this view. Early studies of the effects of trade policies and agreements from the 1970s and 1980s, for example, tended to report small effects on trade flows.[7] Later studies that employed gravity-equation-based approaches to analyze the drivers of trade growth—in order to identify the relative contributions of trade policies, reductions in transportation and other trade costs, and income growth or convergence—yielded mixed results. The best-known and most controversial such analysis is perhaps the 2004 study by Andrew

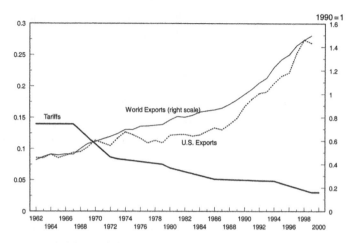

Figure 1.5
Manufacturing export share of GDP and manufacturing tariff rates.
Source: Kei-Mu Yi, "Can Vertical Specialization Explain the Growth of World Trade?," *Journal of Political Economy* 111, no. 1 (February 2003): 54.

Rose that claimed that GATT or WTO membership had no discernible effects on trade volumes.[8]

The most influential academic paper to argue that trade policy, specifically tariffs, could not account for the recent wave of globalization was published by Kei-Mu Yi in the *Journal of Political Economy* in 2003.[9] Yi rightly notes that the sharp decline in US tariff levels following World War II had more or less run its course by the 1970s, after which point tariffs continued to decline but at a much slower rate—and yet US exports and global trade levels continued to grow and even accelerate. Figure 1.5 illustrates Yi's main point: by the early 1990s, US tariff levels had nearly plateaued at a very low level, just as US exports and global trade volumes were entering the period of hyperglobalization. If the "age of globalization" was catalyzed by the post–World War II period's dramatic decline in global tariff levels, what explains this dramatic acceleration in US exports once US tariff levels had effectively leveled out close to zero? Unless export levels were extremely responsive to small tariff reductions (i.e., unless the tariff elasticity was much higher than most economists would believe), Yi argued that something other than trade policy must have been driving these trends. Intuitively, many economists at the time concluded that the "other factor" driving hyperglobalization was technology—namely the falling costs of transportation and communication.

While technological developments surely contributed to the acceleration of global trade in the 1990s, the data tell a much more nuanced story.[10] On the top panel of figure 1.6, for instance, it is clear that the use of new information and communications technologies (ICTs)—particularly cell phones and the internet—increased dramatically starting around 1992, quickly overtaking "landline" telephone subscriptions, which by the late 2000s began to decline. The bottom panel of figure 1.6, meanwhile, shows the declining costs of transportation and communication throughout the twentieth century. Between 1920 and 2015, the costs of computer storage, sea freight shipping, round-trip airfare between New York City and London, and a three-minute

---

→

Figure 1.6
Above: ICT use, 1960–2017. *Below:* Transport and communication costs, 1920–2015. *Note:* In the top panel, data are available for over two hundred countries. Mobile cellular subscriptions per one hundred persons may be over a hundred as some people may have several cell phones. In the bottom panel, for each indicator the cost is reported as one hundred for the first year with data. *Source:* World Bank, *World Development Report 2020: Trading for Development in the Age of Global Value Chains* (Washington, DC: World Bank, 2019), 20, using data from ITU's World Telecommunication/ICT Indicators database for the top panel, and for the bottom panel, based on Jean-Paul Rodrigue, Claude Comtois, and Brian Slack, *The Geography of Transport Systems*, 4th ed. (New York: Routledge, 2017).

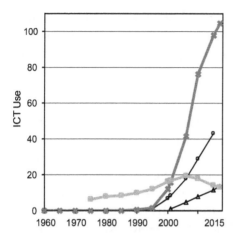

— Individuals using the Internet (% of global population)
— Fixed broadband subscriptions (per 100 people)
— Mobile cellular subscriptions (per 100 people)
— Fixed telephone subscriptions (per 100 people)

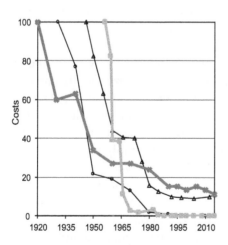

— Air fare (New York London round trip, 1946 = 100)
— Telephone call (3 minutes, New York London, 1931 = 100)
— Sea freight rates (port and maritime charges per ton, 1920 = 100)
— Computers (storage costs per megabyte, 1956 = 100)

telephone call between the same two cities all declined sharply—which likewise seems to support the general notion that technological developments enabled the twentieth century's dramatic increases in global trade levels.

A closer look at the bottom panel, however, shows that these cost declines had all more or less leveled out by the 1970s or early 1980s. They continued to decline thereafter, but like US tariff levels in figure 1.5, the declines were much less pronounced. During the 1990s, they barely changed at all, and sea freight rates increased slightly during the first half of the decade. Based on these data, it would be hard to attribute the sharp growth in global trade levels—which happened mostly in the 1990s—to declining transportation and communication costs alone. In other words, declining tariffs may not have had a major effect on hyperglobalization, but neither was it driven solely by a magical "other factor" like technology. So then, what else was going on?

In fact, trade policy has played a much more important role in fostering trade growth than the recent consensus gives credit—both in terms of tariffs and nontariff barriers. Three factors can help understand why this is the case.

First, it is important to recognize the diversity in tariff reductions across countries. The line graphs in figure 1.7, for example, compare tariffs that were applied in developed countries versus developing countries between 1948 and 2016. ("Applied" tariffs simply refer to the effective duties actually imposed by a given country, and they can be lower than "statutory" or "legal" tariffs established by customs tariff laws; "applied" tariffs are typically passed by governments due to economic reasons for a limited or indeterminate period of time. A good example is US-China trade in the late twentieth century: even before China joined the WTO in 2001, it enjoyed a special trade status in the United States whereby Congress annually approved

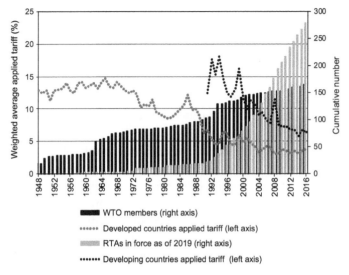

Figure 1.7
Tariffs and trade agreements, 1948–2016. *Note:* The figure plots tariffs computed as simple averages for developed and developing countries. Prior to 1988, the developed country sample covers thirty-five countries, including twenty-one industrialized countries (Argentina, Australia, Austria-Hungary, Canada, Chile, Cuba, Denmark, France, Germany, Greece, Italy, New Zealand, Norway, Portugal, Russia, Serbia, Spain, Sweden, the United Kingdom, the United States, and Uruguay) and fourteen developing countries at the time (Brazil, Burma [now Myanmar], Ceylon [now Sri Lanka], China, Colombia, Egypt, India, Indonesia, Japan, Mexico, Peru, the Philippines, Siam [now Thailand], and Turkey). After 1988, developed countries are defined as high-income countries and developing countries as not high-income countries based on the World Bank's 2018 country classification. *Sources:* World Bank, *World Development Report 2020: Trading for Development in the Age of Global Value Chains* (Washington, DC: World Bank, 2019), 20, based on Richard Baldwin, "Global Supply Chains: Why They Emerged, Why They Matter, and Where They Are Going," CEPR Discussion Paper 9103, Centre for Economic Policy Research, August 2012, https://cepr.org/active/publications/discussion_papers/dp.php?dpno=9103. Data for regional trade agreements (RTAs) and WTO members from the WTO's RTAs database. Tariff data prior to 1988 are from Michael Clemens and Jeffrey Williamson, "Why Did the Tariff-Growth Correlation Change after 1950?," *Journal of Economic Growth* 9, no. 1 (March 2004): 5–46. Tariff data for subsequent years are from the World Bank's World Development Indicators database using country-level weighted applied tariffs for all products.

applied tariffs on Chinese imports that were much lower than the US statutory tariffs it would have faced, as we discuss further in section 2.3.1.) The figure shows how applied tariffs in developed countries have declined only marginally in recent decades, and certainly since 1992—which is consistent with Yi's observation. But in developing countries applied tariffs have declined quite sharply, especially since the early 1990s.

Second, it is important to consider the role of tariffs in GVCs, which we will explore more in the next section. While GVCs have existed for centuries, they grew rapidly in the 1990s as technological advances and lower trade barriers motivated firms to specialize in different stages of value chains and move production processes across national borders to enhance efficiency and productivity. Indeed, Yi highlights GVCs—which in his terminology correspond to "vertical specialization." GVCs reflect another dimension of technology's impacts on trade. But GVCs also had the effect of amplifying trade policy. Specifically, the fragmentation of production magnified the impact of tariffs and any policies to reduce them: now that products, parts, and components crisscrossed borders multiple times during production, even low tariffs could add up across multiple countries—and likewise, even a small decrease in tariffs could have big cumulative effects on trade. In other words, it is not implausible to think that the tariff elasticity was very large after all, precisely because of the technological developments manifested by GVCs. As Yi points out, it is the interaction of tariffs with technology that explains the large tariff elasticity.

Third, declining nontariff trade barriers—a factor largely overlooked by the recent consensus—also played an important role in facilitating growth in trade. The global trade architecture underwent a significant expansion in the late twentieth century. The bar graphs in figure 1.7 above, for instance, show how WTO membership increased steadily and substantially over the second half of the twentieth century, and how the signing of regional trade agreements has increased dramatically since the early 1990s—starting at precisely the same time as the onset of the hyperglobalization wave. While it is impossible to measure the precise impact of WTO membership and regional trade agreements on trade levels, the aforementioned trends offer some plausible links. As a standard-setting body that promotes trade liberalization, for instance, the WTO has attracted membership by a large number of developing countries—the same country group that has seen its applied tariff levels decline sharply since the 1990s. The WTO's food safety and sanitary standards offer just one example of how these trends influence global trade: coming into force in January 1995, the Agreement on the Application of Sanitary and Phytosanitary Measures (or "SPS Agreement") served to reassure advanced countries that food produced elsewhere did not put human, animal, or plant life and health at risk, assuaging consumer concerns and ultimately promoting trade in food products between countries of vastly different levels of development. Moreover, regional trade agreements (many of which involved developing countries in recent decades) are often drafted to reflect WTO-style standards or are made feasible because all signatories are already WTO members.

Likewise, the stability and predictability generated by WTO membership, spelling out a system of rules that all participants must follow, was instrumental in fostering investments that were important for the emergence of GVCs. While bilateral or regional trade agreements can also help trade flourish in this way, the distinctive feature of modern GVCs is their global nature; US parts and services shipped to China, for example, are used in products exported to Europe, Africa, or even back to the United States, crisscrossing the borders of countries and entire continents. This truly global trade of inputs, intermediates, and final goods, moving in all directions at once around the entire world, is bolstered by systems of stability and predictability that extend to the entire globe.

Of course, it is possible that other factors could have sparked the period of hyperglobalization. Indeed, not *all* WTO initiatives were beneficial to all participating countries; the highly controversial Trade-Related Aspects of International Property Protection (TRIPS), for instance, created the impression that the WTO was captive to the interests of multinational conglomerates in order to serve the interests of advanced countries at the expense of developing ones.[11] Trade growth is certainly feasible without multilateralism: many industry standards, for example—from cell phone communication protocols and the internet to best practice production standards established by the International Organization for Standardization (ISO)—have evolved without government intervention, though they are often supported by WTO involvement. Several multinational firms have also imposed "responsible sourcing" rules on themselves in response to market pressures (i.e., demands from consumers in advanced countries). The very formation of multinationals and the emergence and growth of GVCs were aided in part by legal provisions in regional and bilateral trade agreements as well as by regional political blocs like the European Union. Nonetheless, it is clear that hyperglobalization was closely linked to the growth of GVCs and developing countries' increased participation in *global* trade, and it is highly unlikely that these trends would have grown so much and so fast during the 1990s and 2000s without multilateral agreements like the WTO. When goods and services are traded across the entire globe, regional agreements do not suffice; only multilaterism can offer the degree of stability and predictability required for global trade to flourish.

In sum, the post–World War II "age of globalization" and the period of hyperglobalization in the late twentieth century had many drivers. But contrary to the recent consensus, trade policy—especially the creation of a predictably stable global trading environment—was at least as important as technological development, the effects of which may have been overestimated until recently. Ironically, it took the rise in trade tensions that ultimately culminated in the recent trade war between the United States and China for economists to once again appreciate the importance of the relatively open and stable global trading system we had been taking for granted. As we will see in the sections that follow, the short-run economic costs of the trade war appear to have been modest—but its long-run consequences on trade and investment as well as its political ramifications may turn out to be much more severe.[12]

1.3   Why Claims of a "Secular Slowdown" in Trade Are Premature

International trade has slowed quite substantially since the global financial crisis. Some economists and policy makers have characterized the slowdown as secular (or long-term), suggesting that the fragmentation of global production through GVCs may have finally run its course. Fragmentation clearly does have limits; the automotive industry, for instance—in which GVCs are particularly prevalent—can split car production into thousands of individual parts and components across thousands of different firms and

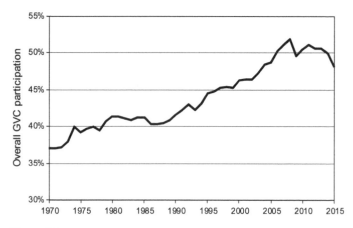

Figure 1.8
GVC trade, 1970–2015. *Note:* GVC participation measures used in this and subsequent figures throughout the monograph follow the methodology from Alessandro Borin and Michele Mancini, "Follow the Value Added: Bilateral Gross Export Accounting" (Temi di discussione [Economic Working Paper] 1026, Economic Research and International Relations Area, Bank of Italy, 2015); Alessandro Borin and Michele Mancini, "Measuring What Matters in Global Value Chains and Value-Added Trade" (Policy Research Working Paper 8804, World Bank, Washington, DC, April 2019), https://openknowledge.worldbank.org/handle/10986/31533. *Sources:* World Bank, *World Development Report 2020: Trading for Development in the Age of Global Value Chains* (Washington, DC: World Bank, 2019), 20 using data from Eora26 database; Borin and Mancini, "Measuring What Matters in Global Value Chains and Value-Added Trade"; Robert Johnson and Guillermo Noguera, "A Portrait of Trade in Value Added over Four Decades," *Review of Economics and Statistics* 99, no. 5 (December 2017): 896–911.

markets, but eventually no further specialization will be possible. Is that what's actually happening? Has the global trading system reached some fundamental technological constraint? Figure 1.8 suggests that it may have, showing how the share of GVCs in total global trade collapsed after 2008, recovering briefly but then continuing its decline. If this slowdown is secular, it could have major impacts on international trade and the global economy; GVCs still account for nearly half of all trade and in many ways typify the last few decades of globalization.

This view is far from conclusive, however, and there are many good reasons to believe that international fragmentation may actually still have a way to go. The issue is hotly debated among economists, with a large and growing academic literature that utilizes a range of different measures and databases. Often, different measures can produce different findings. For instance, many economists measure GVC trade by tracking trade in intermediate goods, which are inputs used to produce a finished product. The gray dotted line in figure 1.9, for example, shows trade in intermediate goods as a percentage of world GDP between 1990 and 2017, with the bottom graph showing the same data magnified to the period 2010–2017. Intermediate trade follows a similar trend as the total GVC trade: collapsing in 2008, recovering briefly, and then continuing to decline after 2013—again suggesting the possibility of a secular slowdown. But this measure includes trade in commodities, the price of which can fluctuate wildly for many regions, often for reasons that have nothing to do with GVCs themselves. By contrast, many economists also measure GVC trade by tracking trade in parts and components, which excludes trade in commodities. The solid black line in figure 1.9 shows trade in parts and components, following a smoother trend line since 2008 with no indication of long-term slowdown.

Similarly, recent trends in GVC trade have been influenced by China's efforts to rebalance its economy away from the focus on exports toward more domestic production. By virtue of the Chinese economy's size, any shift in it away from GVC participation can have a large effect on the aggregate statistics. Figure 1.10 shows the share

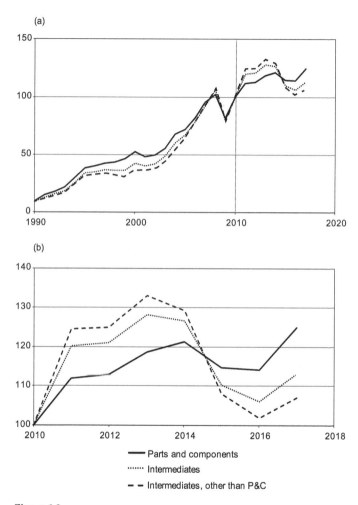

Figure 1.9
(a) Trade in intermediates as well as parts and components, 1990–2017.
(b) Trade in intermediates as well as parts and components, 2010–2017.
Source: Pinelopi Goldberg, "The Future of Trade," IMF Finance and Development, June 2019, 23, https://www.elibrary.imf.org/view/journals/022 /2019/002/022.2019.issue-002-en.xml, using data from UN Comtrade, 2022, http://comtrade.un.org.

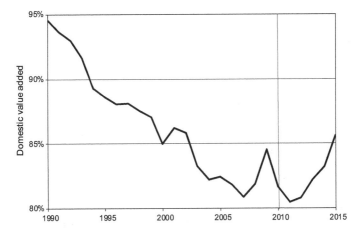

Figure 1.10
China's domestic value added (embodied in exports). *Source:* Pinelopi Goldberg, "The Future of Trade," IMF Finance and Development, June 2019, 22, https://www.elibrary.imf.org/view/journals/022/2019/002/022.2019.issue-002-en.xml, using data from OECD-WTO's TiVA database.

of domestic value embodied in Chinese exports, which declined steadily throughout the 1990s—when China's export-driven growth model supported hyperglobalization—before increasing in the late 2000s and continuing to increase in the years following the global financial crisis. If it continues, China's rebalancing may further dampen GVC trade, but this does not mean that globalization itself has entered a secular slowdown. Of course, anything could happen, but in the current moment, it would be premature to conclude that the slowdown is secular using only a few years of recent data. At a minimum, these graphs cast doubt on the notion that fragmentation has reached some technological constraint that will prevent future trade growth.

1.4   How the Recent Backlash May Still Engender Deglobalization or "Slowbalization"

While recent claims of a secular slowdown in global trade may be premature, the world is clearly experiencing a significant backlash against globalization. Ultimately, this backlash and the uncertainty it provokes may have greater implications for the future of trade than any other factor. There are numerous examples of backlash—particularly in developed countries, where free trade and immigration (the topics most frequently linked in globalization debates) are now highly divisive political and social issues. The backlash appears broad and persistent, not constrained to any single country or administration. In the United States, many of the protectionist policies and tariff increases implemented by the Trump administration have thus far been maintained by the Biden administration. In the United Kingdom, Brexit has been the focal issue across multiple parliamentary elections. While governments in continental Europe have not to date embraced protectionism, several influential politicians or political parties have taken strong antitrade or anti-EU positions—for example, Marine Le Pen in France, the Alternative for Germany (AfD) party in Germany, or Viktor Orbán in Hungary—and there is significant skepticism toward immigration in many EU member countries. Perhaps most strikingly, for years the WTO has been locked in a series of existential crises between members that were only exacerbated by COVID-19, incapacitating the institution's core functions of negotiation, dispute settlement, and trade policy notifications. One result of these trade tensions and the general climate thwarting international cooperation is a recent slowdown in new regional trade agreements. Figure 1.11 shows the number of new regional trade agreements formed by year,

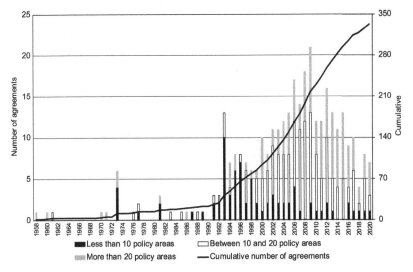

Figure 1.11
Number of policy areas covered in regional trade agreements, 1958–2020. *Source:* Claudia Hofmann, Alberto Osnago, and Michele Ruta, "Horizontal Depth: A New Database on the Content of Preferential Trade Agreements" (Policy Research Working Paper No. 7981, World Bank, Washington, DC, February 2017), https://openknowledge.worldbank.org /handle/10986/26148.

highlighting a slowdown during the 2010s and a significant drop in 2018.[13]

Discontent with globalization is of course not a new phenomenon, and similar backlashes have occurred throughout recent history. In the late 1980s and early 1990s, for example, the United States and Japan experienced trade tensions that were in many ways quite similar to what is occurring today. At the time, there were concerns about Japan's export growth, the rapid success of its automobile and other industries in global markets, and its restrictions on market access. Other countries (led by the United States) worried about the detrimental effects that these factors would have on their domestic industries and workers, primarily low-skilled workers—and at the time, many warned that trade tensions with Japan could lead to the demise of the global system of open trade. Of course, such severe concerns were ultimately not justified. While the trade conflict with Japan did lead to some policy actions by the United States, including voluntary export restraints (VERs) in the auto industry, the trade tensions were eventually resolved in the years that followed, which coincided with the era of the WTO and hyperglobalization. When global trade tensions reemerged between the United States and China in recent years, many economists and policy makers presumed that a similar scenario as in the late 1980s and early 1990s was unfolding. They presumed that the harsh rhetoric and hardball trade negotiation tactics between major economic powers would be a temporary phenomenon that could be swiftly resolved, perhaps resulting in another era of hyperglobalization. It is now clear, however, that something is different this time. Tough talk has escalated into tangible tensions, and policy makers have responded to these tensions with concrete trade policy actions. We have entered a period of heightened uncertainty, which may in fact lead to a new era of deglobalization.

Yet it should also be noted that the backlash against globalization is still relatively new, and that the world—the above concerns notwithstanding—has not as of yet entered into a period of sustained or widespread deglobalization. As many economists have pointed out in recent years, while the "age of globalization" and the hyperglobalization that followed are characterized by free trade, certain sectors of the global economy have more or less always been characterized by protection. Even before the current backlash, for example, agricultural trade was highly restricted, and trade in services has seen limited liberalization. Even within the European Union, which is perhaps the world's most integrated market, integration extends mostly to trade in goods rather than trade in services. Likewise, even though tariff levels reached historically low levels in recent decades, there are many so-called behind-the-border measures that limit trade. Economists traditionally referred to such policy measures as nontariff trade barriers, but they have evolved into something more extensive—often involving regulations that impose many restrictions on trade between countries and introduce significant domestic distortions that interfere with trade.[14]

Considering these factors, it is perhaps not surprising that the aggregate effects of the recent trade tensions appear to be rather small. Figure 1.12, for example, reflects

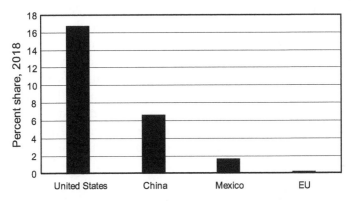

Figure 1.12
Goods imports impacted by new tariffs. *Sources:* Adapted from Pablo Fajgelbaum, Pinelopi Goldberg, Patrick Kennedy, and Amit Khandelwal, "The Return to Protectionism," *Quarterly Journal of Economics* 135, no. 1 (February 2020): 1–55; Pablo Fajgelbaum, Pinelopi Goldberg, Patrick Kennedy, Amit Khandelwal, and Daria Taglioni, "The US-China Trade War and Global Reallocations" (NBER Working Paper No. 29562, National Bureau of Economic Research, Cambridge, MA, December 2021), https://www.nber.org/papers/w29562.

analysis that my coauthors and I published in 2020.[15] It
shows that the share of goods imports affected by new
tariffs is approximately just 17 percent in the United States,
7 percent in China, 2 percent in Mexico, and less than 1
percent in the European Union. In terms of absolute size,
given the magnitude of total global trade, these numbers
are quite small.

To understand why the aggregate losses from the recent
protection wave appear small, it is useful to understand
how economists typically quantify the aggregate gains
from trade, meaning the gains accrued to a country's
economy as a whole. Only two variables are needed: the
country's share of the total expenditure on domestically
produced goods and the overall elasticity of trade, or how
responsive trade levels are to changes in the price of goods,
which can be estimated using one of several established
methods. The relationship between these two variables
and the aggregate gains from trade—named the ACR formula after economists Costas Arkolakis, Arnaud Costinot,
and Andres Rodríguez-Clare, who developed it in 2012—is
consistent across a very large class of trade models that use
different and often more complicated methods.[16] The ACR
formula shows that the aggregate gains from trade (or the
losses from increased protection) are often small, especially
for large economies, and especially those with a large share
of domestic expenditure. This makes intuitive sense: if a
large economy like the United States or United Kingdom
depends less on imports and exports, its aggregate gains
or losses from more or less trade—despite some potential
efficiency gains or losses—will probably not be huge. Even
in China, the loss from the new tariffs is relatively small
because China is a large economy.

Of course, this does not mean that the recent trade tensions have not had significant costs. While static trade
models capture its short-run aggregate effects (i.e., on

prices, trade flows, and their direct implications for welfare), they do not capture the so-called dynamic gains or losses realized over longer periods through indirect and often complex channels. For instance, cross-border trade can enhance productivity by fostering the exchange of ideas across countries; exposure to import competition can drive innovation and encourage the adoption of efficient business practices and elimination of market distortions; and the stability and security trade needs to thrive can encourage international cooperation and promote peace. In fact, trade agreements are often signed with political objectives in mind; the 1951 proposal to establish the European Coal and Steel Community, for instance, which French minister of foreign affairs Robert Schuman declared would "make war not only unthinkable but materially impossible," lit the spark for European integration.

Such long-term and indirect effects may be elusive to empirical work, but this does not mean that they are unimportant. In fact, their influence could be orders of magnitude larger than the static effects of trade. This is especially likely in the context of the recent trade tensions between the United States and China, which have resulted in heightened uncertainty in the global economy and doubts about the future of international cooperation. Uncertainty is detrimental to the realization of trade's potential long-run gains, as these gains typically rely on long-term investments—both economic and political in nature—that are only possible in stable and predictable environments. Moreover, there is extensive evidence showing that the distributional effects of the recent trade tensions have been considerable given that consumers typically bear the cost of tariffs. In the United States, for example, farmers in the agricultural regions were the most adversely affected by new tariffs; the retaliatory measures by China (and the European Union, to a certain extent) specifically targeted regions with strong Republican support, which is the case for many areas that produce agricultural products. In some respects, economists' preoccupation with the aggregate effects in our trade models have led us to forget that international trade is much more about distributional gains and losses—which is the primary focus of this monograph, and will be explored in greater detail in the next section.

While the recent tensions may not have had large aggregate effects on global trade so far, the more significant concern—among commentators, policy makers, and international institutions—is the heightened uncertainty they have provoked. Increased uncertainty has detrimental long-run effects on investment, which goes hand in hand with GVCs. Given the central role of GVCs in the global economy, sustained uncertainty could cause important shifts, such as GVC relocation, which could impact global growth prospects. If the current trade tensions do not get resolved, and the world enters a sustained period of trade conflict and instability, these shifts could ripple through the global economy. Even this, though, might not have a large aggregate impact on global growth, beyond a temporary slowdown and some marginal efficiency and productivity losses. It is highly unlikely that today's advanced economies will revert to autarky or complete economic independence without engaging in international trade; in the medium to long run, the more plausible developments are a reorientation of trade flows and the strengthening of regional trading blocks.

Indeed, the findings of a new paper by myself and several coauthors confirm this view.[17] Examining the effects of the recent trade war between the United States and China on "bystander" countries—or countries that were not *directly* affected by the tariff increases (i.e., countries other than the United States and China)—we find that the global exports of many of these countries actually increased as a result of the trade war. In fact, the rise in their global exports was large enough to offset the collapse of trade between the United States and China, so that by the end of 2019, global trade levels in the products most affected by the new tariffs had *increased* in response to the trade war. This unexpected finding suggests that despite the heightened uncertainty, global trade did not collapse. Rather, it was reoriented away from the United States and China toward other countries that saw an opportunity to increase their global presence. Of course, these bystander countries have not been immune to the uncertainties exacerbated by elevated trade tensions. Anecdotally, their rising trade levels have been accompanied by rising anxiety that their countries would be the next victims of the trade war to be hit with tariffs. Likewise, these countries have in general become less certain of how much they should trust in or rely on the global trading system. Nonetheless, the implication is that recent trends may not signify the end of globalization but rather the onset of a different kind of globalization.

In the long run, the most severe adverse effects of deglobalization or slowbalization would likely be felt by today's low-income countries, especially in Africa, which are not yet fully integrated into the world trading system. For small economies that do not have a sustainably large domestic market (as large economies like India or China do), trade is an important prerequisite for growth, as I argue in recent work with Tristan Reed of the World Bank.[18] The future growth prospects of small, low-income countries rely heavily on their connection to the global trading system because trade—despite its caveats and shortcomings—and especially trade with more advanced economies, is still the only viable path we know for such countries to achieve rapid economic growth. If this path suddenly forecloses, there is no obvious alternative. The growth failure of small developing countries might not affect the aggregate global growth statistics given their relative size, but a large portion of the world's population would suddenly have much worse prospects for escaping poverty and achieving prosperity in the foreseeable future.

Of course, this analysis predates the onset of COVID-19—which has caused trade to collapse among all countries, rich or poor. Ironically, the pandemic itself is a manifestation of a different kind of globalization: the globalization of health. The health and economic crises of COVID-19 have in turn led to a second backlash and a new set of arguments against trade. This time, the arguments are focused on concerns about the *perceived* lack of GVC resilience, which have led to even louder calls for protectionism and self-sufficiency. These developments have only exacerbated uncertainty about the future of globalization. A key question, then, given the current environment, is whether the recent tensions, backlash, and demands for protection are just small blips amid the unstoppable and irreversible march of globalization—or whether we are actually witnessing the dawn of a new era of sustained deglobalization or slowbalization.

The answer, I believe, will ultimately depend on policy choices. If you believe that the recent slowdown was not solely driven by technological factors, but that trade policy in fact played a large role, then it follows that a slowdown is not unstoppable or inevitable, and that trade policy can in principle reverse it. The future of globalization—or its undoing—will depend on how policy makers and political leaders around the world deal with these pressing challenges over the next few years.

This, of course, invites yet another question: What caused the backlash and tensions in the first place?

2   Causes of the Backlash

2.1   Evolving Attitudes toward Trade

The central second section of this monograph dives head-long into the backlash itself, specifically its many causes and drivers—which of course are broadly summarized in the monograph's title: *The Unequal Effects of Globalization.* As will be seen, this is primarily a story about inequality and its diverse manifestations in today's global economy.

Unpacking the causes of the backlash against globalization begins with an important puzzle: How did it gain steam during the last several years, during a period of unprecedented global prosperity? In the United States before COVID-19, for example, unemployment had reached fifty-year lows, the stock market was enjoying a period of historic and sustained strength, and the average consumer actually felt good about these factors according to surveys. So why now? Before we begin to answer this question, it is helpful to consider how far public opinion has shifted over time.

A useful source of information for public opinion on globalization is the Pew Global Attitudes Survey, which collects information on people's attitudes on key issues in many countries across the income spectrum. In 2002, a

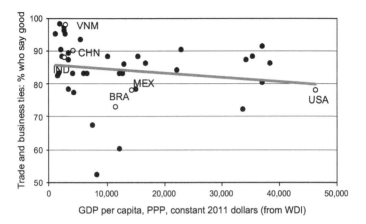

Figure 2.1
Attitudes toward free trade, 2002. *Source:* Nina Pavcnik, "The Impact of Trade on Inequality in Developing Countries," *Jackson Hole Economic Policy Symposium Proceedings* (August 2017): 72.

question on the survey was, "Do you think trade and business ties between countries are good for the economy?" Figure 2.1 plots the 2002 survey results for this question alongside country income levels. Each dot represents a country, with each country's survey response on the vertical y-axis and its income (according to GDP per capita, in constant 2011 terms) on the horizontal x-axis. The richer the country, the farther to the right it is on the graph, and the higher the dot, the higher the share of people in that country who said trade is good for the economy in 2002. Note that the scale of the vertical axis starts at 50 percent, and most of the dots fall between 80 and 90 percent; these are very high numbers, suggesting that most people in most countries in 2002 thought trade and business ties were good for the economy as a whole. The relationship between income and survey response is slightly negative, suggesting that everyone appreciates trade, but poorer

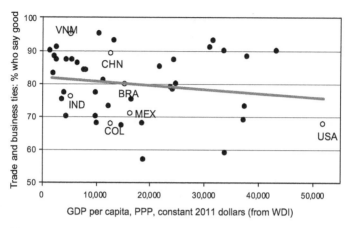

Figure 2.2
Attitudes toward free trade, 2014. *Source:* Nina Pavcnik, "The Impact of Trade on Inequality in Developing Countries," *Jackson Hole Economic Policy Symposium Proceedings* (August 2017): 72.

countries appreciate it even more. Vietnam and China, two poorer countries known to have benefited from free trade, clearly valued free trade greatly in 2002.

To see how general attitudes about trade have shifted over time, figure 2.2 plots the same graph using Pew survey responses from 2014—a few years before the recent trade tensions began emerging. While the overall trend is slightly more negative, it is striking that all countries are still above 50 percent in their survey responses: most people in most countries still thought trade was good for the economy in 2014. In the United States, the share of people who thought trade was good for the economy decreased from nearly 80 percent in 2002 to slightly more than 65 percent in 2014, but this still reflects a healthy majority of the respondents. Notably, the 2014 graph shows much more dispersion among the dots, suggesting that the diversity of views about trade had widened between countries.

While the share of positive responses fell dramatically in some countries (e.g., India), many other countries are still highly in favor of trade (e.g., Vietnam and China). Interestingly, Latin American countries (e.g., Mexico or Columbia) appear much more lukewarm about trade. But overall, even in 2014, global public opinion suggests that most people still think trade is good for the economy as a whole.

What about more specific opinions about trade? Figure 2.3 uses the same country income data to plot survey responses to the 2014 Pew Global Attitudes Survey questions about trade and labor market outcomes. The questions on the survey were, "Does trade raise wages, or does it lower wages?" and "Does trade create jobs, or does it destroy jobs?" Since these questions are much more focused on labor market outcomes instead of general views about whether trade is good or bad for an economy, a very different picture emerges. For instance, there is a strong relationship between per capita income and perceptions about trade's labor effects. The richer the country, the more pronounced the beliefs that trade lowers wages and destroys jobs. Likewise, the poorer the country, the stronger the perceptions that trade increases wages and creates jobs. Combining these survey results with what we just saw in figure 2.2, the contrast is striking: in high-income countries like the United States, many respondents feel that trade is bad for the labor market despite it being good for the economy as whole, whereas in developing countries like Vietnam, China, India, Brazil, and Mexico, trade is viewed as positive for the economy and workers alike.

This contrast suggests a potential answer to why the backlash against globalization may be occurring now: the effects of globalization are unequal across countries, but also perhaps within countries. As noted in the previous section, the aggregate economy-wide effects of trade are typically quite small; ultimately, international trade—as well as public perceptions about it, and the policies that stem from those perceptions—is much more about distributional gains and losses.

There is mounting evidence in the economics literature that attitudes toward trade are strongly correlated with these distributional effects. A 2005 paper by Anna Maria Mayda and Dani Rodrik, for instance, analyzes a rich cross-country data set on attitudes toward trade, and finds that they are highly correlated with a range of sociodemographic indicators, including an individual's relative economic status in their country and their skills or human capital.[1] Mayda and Rodrik document that trade preferences are correlated with the sector in which an individual is employed: people in sectors that have a comparative disadvantage—and are hence more likely to be adversely affected by trade—tend to be protectionist; in contrast, people in nontraded sectors whose employment is not directly affected by trade tend to be more protrade.

Similar evidence has emerged for a wide range of countries. For example, a 2022 paper by Esteban Méndez-Chacón and Diana van Patten studies the extent to which economic fundamentals drive attitudes toward trade in Costa Rica: exploiting results from a 2007 national referendum in which citizens voted on whether a free trade agreement (FTA) with the United States should be ratified, they find that people's voting behavior largely depended on the extent of their employers' trade exposure (directly or indirectly via input-output linkages) and that import competition played a key role in explaining votes against the FTA.[2] In the United States, a provocative 2021 paper by Jiwon Choi, Ilyana Kuziemko, Ebonya Washington, and Gavin Wright argues that the 1994 North American Free Trade Agreement (NAFTA) played a major role in the departure

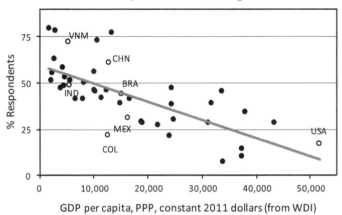

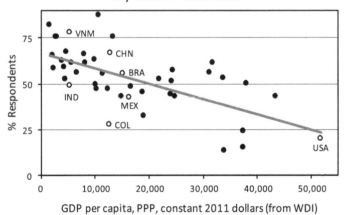

Figure 2.3
Pew Global Attitudes Survey responses about trade and labor market
outcomes, 2014. *Source:* Nina Pavcnik, "The Impact of Trade on Inequality in Developing Countries," *Jackson Hole Economic Policy Symposium
Proceedings* (August 2017): 74.

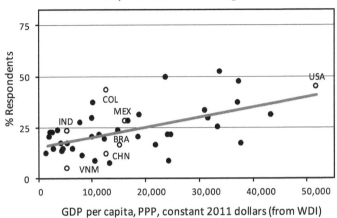

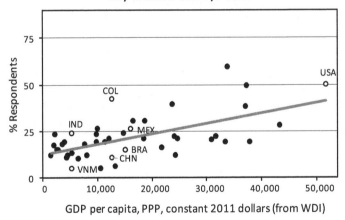

Figure 2.3 (continued)

of less educated white voters from the Democratic Party in counties that were more vulnerable to increased import competition from Mexico.[3] Likewise, two studies—a 2016 paper by Yi Che, Yi Lu, Justin Pierce, Peter Schott, and Zhigang Tao, and a 2020 paper by David Autor, David Dorn, Gordon Hanson, and Kaveh Majlesi—argue that recent US election results were affected by the degree to which a given geographic area was subject to import competition from China.[4] In France and Germany, a 2017 paper by Clément Malgouyres, and a 2015 paper by Christian Dippel, Robert Gold, and Stephan Heblich, respectively, document that greater import competition has resulted in larger vote shares for Far Right political parties.[5] In Great Britain, a 2018 paper by Italo Colantone and Piero Stanig similarly shows that support for Brexit was higher in regions hit harder by exposure to trade in recent decades.[6]

In much of this literature, there is evidence that citizens do care about trade's aggregate effects, namely decreased consumer prices from increased trade. Nevertheless, concern about their own economic welfare as a function of their skills, industry of employment, and location seems to be the primary factor in determining their attitude toward trade. Against this backdrop, the "unequal" effects of trade are likely to have contributed to the recent backlash against openness.

Let us now turn to these unequal effects. What do we have in mind when we talk about inequality? Inequality is an extremely complex phenomenon, with multiple dimensions and approaches for understanding and measuring it. In the context of the issues we are focused on in this monograph, the very simple schematic below is useful for thinking about two major aspects of inequality. *Global inequality* refers to the inequality that would be apparent if we ignored country borders altogether and evaluated the gaps in well-being across the entire global population. Because this measure is affected primarily by how the populations in some large countries (e.g., India and China) fare relative to the populations of other countries, it is often thought of as reflecting inequality between countries. *Within-country inequality* considers a single country at a time. The relationship between trade and inequality is complicated in this case because trade affects the population of a country in two related but different and often contrasting ways: it affects them as *consumers*, through price decreases or increases resulting from more or less trade, and it affects them as *workers*, through trade's effects on labor market outcomes. This schematic offers a useful structure for thinking through the distributional effects of trade. We will start at the broadest level by exploring trade issues through the lens of global inequality.

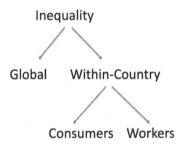

2.2   Trade and Global Inequality: Winners and Losers?

There is substantial evidence and widespread consensus among economists and economic historians that global inequality has decreased dramatically in recent decades, especially in the decades since World War II. In his 2013 book *The Great Escape*, Nobel Prize–winning economist

Angus Deaton highlights today's slowing growth and widening gaps, but also shows that human beings have grown vastly healthier and wealthier during the past 250 years, as billions of people have been lifted out of poverty and sickness following millennia of destitution.[7] Likewise, Branko Milanovic's 2016 book *Global Inequality* shows how rising middle-class incomes in countries like China and India as well as the integration of once-disparate regions, especially in China and East Asia but also eastern Europe, have delivered historic reductions in global inequality.[8] In 2006, the World Bank's flagship annual report, the *World Development Report*, argued that equity and economic prosperity are complementary.[9] Deaton, Milanovic, the World Bank, and many other economists credit our progress in reducing global inequality—especially in recent decades—to the opening of long-closed borders, the growth of trade between countries, and the establishment of the modern global trading system, arguing that more free trade and migration would reduce global inequality even further.

This view, however, raises the question of whether there is a trade-off between global inequality and within-country inequality. The most explicit illustration of this point is the so-called elephant curve, first developed by Christoph Lakner and Branko Milanovic in 2016.[10] Figure 2.4 reproduces their original graph, which plots the income growth rate against the various percentiles of the global income distribution—called a growth incidence curve—between 1988 and 2008.[11] For each income percentile on the horizontal x-axis, the vertical y-axis shows the income growth rate for that particular percentile. (The hand-drawn lines beneath the graph were added later by Caroline Freund to charmingly highlight the data's elephantine shape.) While the graph does show the high growth rate captured by the world's top 1 percent—and the extremely low growth rate

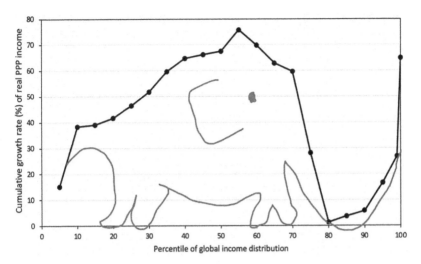

Figure 2.4
The (old) elephant curve: Global growth incidence curve, 1988–2008.
Source: Christoph Lakner and Branko Milanovic, "Global Income Distribution: From the Fall of the Berlin Wall to the Great Recession," *World Bank Economic Review* 30, no. 2 (2016): 203–232. Elephant added by Rada Pavlova, adapted from Caroline Freund.

experienced by people around the eightieth and ninetieth percentile—when Lakner and Milanovic first published it, their primary aim was to show that growth between 1988 and 2008 brought remarkable reductions in global inequality and poverty. This point is supported by the fact that while income growth rates are positive and relatively high for most percentiles in the income distribution, they are particularly high for those in the lower and middle sections, suggesting that the world's poorer groups benefited the most from growth in this period.

Figure 2.5 shows a recent update to the elephant curve, using data from 1980 through 2016, by a group of researchers including Thomas Piketty, Emmanuel Saez, and Gabriel

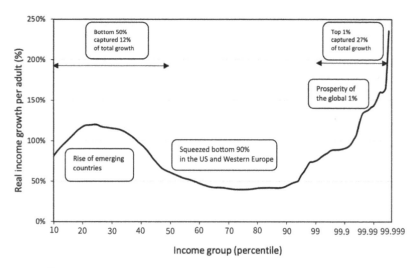

Figure 2.5
The (new) elephant curve: Total income growth by percentile across all world regions, 1980–2016. *Source:* Facundo Alvaredo, Lucas Chancel, Thomas Piketty, Emmanuel Saez, and Gabriel Zucman, eds., *World Inequality Report 2018* (Paris: World Inequality Lab, 2018), 13, https://wir2018.wid.world.

Zucman—economists who have worked extensively on income inequality in the United States using tax data.[12] The update produces a very different graph with very different implications. First, by expanding the ninety-ninetieth income percentile along the horizontal x-axis and increasing the vertical y-axis to 250 percent income growth, this new curve highlights that the world's top 1 percent has captured 27 percent of the total income growth over this nearly four-decade period—a truly huge share. The bottom 50 percent of the income distribution still captured 12 percent of the total growth, but this is a much smaller share and less broadly shared across the middle-income percentiles than in Lakner and Milanovic's earlier graph.

The differences between the two elephant curves can be explained by several methodological differences between the two graphs, including the wider time period, but the most important distinction is that the updated curve is based on income tax data, whereas Lakner and Milanovic's curve was based on survey data.[13] Using income tax data allowed the authors to capture the top end of the income distribution with much greater clarity. When using surveys, many people at these top income levels do not respond—and even when they do, their income gets coded as simply "very high." If you are interested in showing how inequality is driven by the world's top income earners' disproportionate capture of global income growth, the updated elephant curve illustrates that point in a very clear and compelling way.

On the other hand, if you are interested in showing that the world's poor have benefited tremendously from economic growth in recent decades—and have done so partly at the expense of certain middle-income earners—then the lower sections of the income distribution in both figures illustrate this point very well. Especially in the updated elephant curve, people in the bottom deciles—the world's poor, located mostly in developing countries and emerging markets—experienced as much as 125 percent income growth from 1980 to 2016. Yet even as this suggests a reduction in global poverty and inequality, people in the sixtieth, seventieth, eightieth, and ninetieth deciles—corresponding to advanced countries' middle classes—experienced substantially lower income growth during the same period. While neither elephant curve reflects negative income growth—real incomes rise in both figures across the entire range of the global income distribution—what matters for the evolution of inequality is not income growth but rather the *relative* income growth of one group compared to others. In addition to showing that the world's poor and superwealthy benefited, the new elephant curve suggests that (in relative terms) they did so at the expense of the middle classes, especially in the United States and western Europe. The two appear to go hand in hand, raising an important question: Is this trade-off—between being open, embracing globalization, and using the resulting gains to reduce worldwide poverty and lessen global inequality versus nurturing middle-class growth—avoidable or inevitable?

One way to begin answering this question is to take a closer look at the decline in global poverty after World War II. Figure 2.6 shows the declining number of people living in extreme poverty (measured as those earning less than $1.90 per day, adjusted for purchasing power parity) during the recent decades—focusing on the period since 1990, when hyperglobalization started—as well as forecasted data through 2030. (Note: the figure incorporates estimates from late 2020 of increases to poverty head counts due to COVID-19.) The graph shows a sharp decline in poverty across most regions during the 1990s and 2000s. While recent evidence suggests that the pace of poverty reduction slowed in the 2010s—and that COVID-19 reversed progress altogether in 2020 by pushing tens of millions of people into poverty—the overall trend is that enormous progress has been made on the global goal of eliminating extreme poverty.[14] There were many contributors to this progress, but it is worth considering the role that increased trade played.

The most dramatic decreases in poverty in figure 2.6 are in East Asia and the Pacific. This progress can mostly be attributed to China, where approximately one billion people have escaped poverty in recent decades. Clearly, China's increased openness to trade during this period

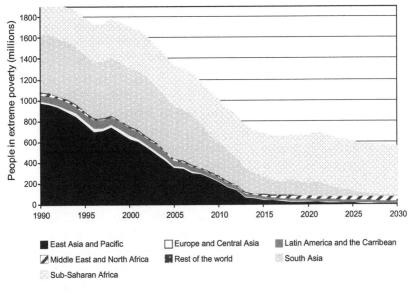

Figure 2.6
The decline in global poverty, 1900–2030. *Source:* Nishant Yonzan, Christoph Lakner, and Daniel Gerszon Mahler, "Projecting Global Extreme Poverty up to 2030: How Close Are We to World Bank's 3% Goal?," World Bank Data Blog, October 9, 2020, https://blogs.worldbank.org /opendata/projecting-global-extreme-poverty-2030-how-close-are-we -world-banks-3-goal.

and its export-driven economic growth model were helpful contributors to this progress. Likewise, large and rapid poverty reductions have been seen in many other countries that embrace globalization, from Korea and Vietnam to eastern Europe.

Notably, the one region that has not seen equivalent progress in recent decades is sub-Saharan Africa—one of the world's least integrated regions, where huge shares of the continent's population are completely disconnected from global markets (and often major domestic urban markets too).[15] The number of poor people living in sub-Saharan Africa (highlighted by the top layer of the graph in figure 2.6) has been more or less stagnant since the 1990s. Today, the majority of the world's poor live in sub-Saharan Africa, and most economic projections suggest that this trend will only continue in future years. Recently, several efforts in sub-Saharan Africa offer promise to improve the region's global integration. For instance, significant investments in transportation and communication infrastructure (including notable efforts by China, often financed through debt agreements that have been severely criticized for their lack of transparency) are creating the roads, ports, and cross-border connections that could enable trade. In addition, the establishment of an African Continental Free Trade Area seeks to promote intra-African trade by harmonizing policies and standards, which could strengthen countries' administrative capabilities for trade (customs, logistics, etc.) and foster economies of scale. These efforts represent enormous progress toward improving Africa's global integration and will perhaps lead to accelerated growth and increased poverty reduction. The long-term effects remain unclear, however, and there are many open questions over whether the region's heavily debt-financed approach to infrastructure development will be economically sustainable in the long run. To date at least, the continent's participation in international trade and GVCs has not kept up with other regions.

While poverty head counts are a very conservative criterion for measuring global prosperity and informing calculations of global inequality, the correlations explored above are strongly suggestive and support a generally positive view of trade's role in recent economic history: increased trade and integration has contributed to dramatic reductions in global poverty, which have led to significant declines in global inequality. But did this global progress against poverty come at the expense of advanced economies and the squeezing of their middle classes, especially in the United States and Europe?

This question features prominently in the recent backlash against globalization and complaints that global trade is not fair. For instance, government and business leaders often complain that large developing countries, namely China and India, routinely abuse their self-determined "special and differential status"—a set of trade-related exceptions in the world trading system available to developing countries, including slower timelines for commitments to tariff reductions and longer timelines for implementing other trade liberalization measures. There are also many complaints that market access in some developing countries is limited, that many developing country governments give subsidies and other unfair advantages to local firms and state-owned enterprises, and that some countries, especially China, engage in forced technology transfer or the outright theft of intellectual property. In addition, as mentioned earlier, trade in services is still highly restricted, and this hurts advanced economies that still enjoy advantages in the services sector. Last but not least, there has been a recent proliferation of "behind-the-border" restrictions that effectively restrict trade.

These concerns have been present for the past two decades, both in the United States and Europe, across political administrations and business cycles, though they became significantly more pronounced in the United States during the Trump administration—contributing to an alarming rise in negative sentiments toward developing countries. It is challenging, however, to differentiate between political posturing and indications of a real problem. In theory, better data should help determine which arguments are grounded. The availability and quality of trade data has increased dramatically in recent decades, but unfortunately the aspects of international trade that are most contentious today are very hard, if not impossible, to measure. Tariffs are easy to measure, but tariffs are not as important as they used to be. The trade restrictions that really matter today—nontariff barriers, "behind-the-border" restrictions, and other regulatory restrictions that effectively restrict cross-border trade—are nearly impossible to measure.

Consider, for example, food safety regulations, which are highly relevant to cross-border trade and especially prevalent in many European countries. How can one determine whether a government's food safety regulations stem from valid health and food quality concerns rather than trade policy designed (in whole or in part) to protect that country's domestic agricultural producers from import competition? The standard data indicators would not indicate the government's underlying rationale for each regulation; even if some food safety regulations are de facto "behind-the-border" trade restrictions, it would be impossible to determine what the true motivation for them was and whether they are justified. In principle, one could check if regulations affect imports more adversely than domestic products and services; if they do, then they should be considered trade restrictions rather than consumer protection. In practice, however, this criterion would be unhelpful for certain types of products that are not produced domestically at all. Chlorinated chicken, for example, is banned in the United Kingdom and the European Union while produced and consumed in the United States. European countries justify the ban on the basis of food safety, but the United States claims that their concerns have no scientific basis and that the ban reflects protectionist motives.

The challenge of differentiating between valid regulations based on the preferences and values of a country's citizens and outright protectionism is present in all cases of product standards. But it is even more acute in the case of labor and safety standards. To improve their living standards, the (once-)poor in China, Vietnam, or Ethiopia may have been content to work long hours at extremely low pay and under harsh, if not dangerous, conditions. One would not expect workers in advanced economies, however, to readily give up their hard-won gains, from minimum wages to other labor market regulations, in order to support the poor in other parts of the world—at least not without putting up the kind of resistance that has led to the rise of economic nationalism in the United States and Europe. To the extent that there is a trade-off between global and within-country inequality, then, this trade-off is most salient in the case of labor standards. But as with product standards, it is hard to draw a clear line between well-founded concerns regarding the safety and welfare of workers and attempts to shield domestic jobs in advanced economies from foreign competition—with the exception of some stark cases, like ethical norms around child labor, where societies seem to have reached a global consensus.

Suffice it to say, then, that the data and the evidence are insufficient and mixed on the question of whether the world's poor have benefited from globalization at the expense of the middle classes in advanced economies. Clearly, there is more going on within countries—which is a useful segue to our second category of inequality.

2.3   Trade and Inequality within Countries: Labor and Prices

As noted, trade affects inequality within countries through two primary channels: the worker channel, through trade's impacts on the labor market, and the consumer channel, through trade's effects on prices. It makes sense to start with the worker channel given that many people (according to the survey responses in figure 2.3) are increasingly concerned that trade may have adverse effects on jobs and wages.

2.3.1 The Unequal Effects on Workers

Economists have long been concerned with inequality in the labor market. Starting in the 1970s, several papers documented that the skill premium—i.e., the gap in wages between skilled and unskilled workers, typically defined in terms of workers' education levels, and thus a key driver of labor market inequality—was increasing in the United States and Europe. By the 1990s, the skill premium was significant.[16] Around that time, the attention also shifted somewhat from low-skill to middle-class jobs. Several economists argued that starting in the 1990s, middle-class workers were increasingly bearing the brunt of adverse effects. Relative to both unskilled and high-skilled workers, middle-class wages were decreasing and jobs were disappearing—a phenomenon called labor market polarization.[17]

What was globalization's role in these developments? A natural starting point for understanding trade's relationship to the increased skill premium is the workhorse model of international trade, the so-called Heckscher-Ohlin model. The model predicts that increased global trade would generate exactly what was observed in the data: since developing countries have an abundance of low-skilled workers and low wages, increasing advanced economies' exposure to trade with developing countries can be expected to have adverse labor market consequences in the advanced economies, including the widening of wage gaps between skilled and unskilled workers.

Nonetheless, throughout the 1990s most economists concluded that trade did not play a large role in these trends.
Rather, the general consensus was that the increasing skill
premium was largely driven by technological developments, with trade playing only a small and secondary role,
mainly through its interaction with technology. This conclusion was based in part on "factor content" studies—or
analyses of trade patterns and production processes that
allow one to compute the labor embodied in a country's
imports and exports—using 1990s' trade data that quanti-
fied the effect of increased import competition in advanced
countries and found it to be small. It was also based on
the observation that developing countries experienced a
pronounced increase in inequality in the 1990s, whereas
traditional trade models would predict the opposite: given
the comparative advantage of developing countries in low-
skill intensive activities, one would expect increased trade
to result in increased low-skill wages and decreased wage
inequality.[18] Studies focusing on increased labor market
polarization during this period likewise concluded that
trade was not the primary driver.

This consensus started shifting in the 2000s, however,
when economists quite suddenly began to see trade as a
potentially important driver of labor market inequality.
But how exactly, and why in the early 2000s? Why did they
fail to find a connection in the 1990s, a period of historically rapid trade growth? These are still open questions,
but there are two potential answers—both having to do
with China, yet the second related to recent shifts in how
economists approach labor market inequality, with a much
greater focus on regional inequality.

China   The last two decades have seen a dramatic decline
in US manufacturing employment. Figure 2.7, reproduced

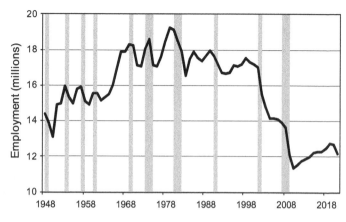

Figure 2.7
US manufacturing unemployment, 1948–2021. *Note:* Shaded bars indicate US recessions according to data from the National Bureau of Economic Research. *Sources:* Justin Pierce and Peter Schott, "The Surprisingly Swift Decline of US Manufacturing Employment," *American Economic Review* 106, no. 7 (July 2016): 1632–1662, with data from US Bureau of Labor Statistics, "All Employees, Manufacturing [CEU3000000001]," FRED, Federal Reserve Bank of St. Louis, https://fred.stlouisfed.org/series /CEU3000000001, October 8, 2022.

from Justin Pierce and Peter Schott's paper in the *American Economic Review*, shows the evolution of US manufacturing employment since 1948. For much of the second half of the twentieth century, manufacturing employment was relatively stable—declining during recessions, but typically bouncing back in the years thereafter. But starting in 2001, it declined precipitously. Approximately 2.9 million US manufacturing jobs were lost between 2001 and 2004, and another 2.5 million were lost during the global financial crisis. Unlike after past recessions, however, there has been no meaningful recovery for US manufacturing. Despite sluggish growth in the early 2010s, manufacturing employment still remains well below historic levels.

To explain these dramatic developments, several economists have noted that China entered the world trading system at precisely the same moment when US manufacturing began to erode—and given the size of its economy, China's entry had large, rapid, and profound effects on global trade dynamics. Pierce and Schott show that two developments during this period were particularly important. First, in 2000, the US government upgraded its trade policy with China.[19] While China had never faced high de facto tariffs from the United States, it did face a high degree of policy uncertainty prior to 2000. Here, a short digression on US trade policy is in order. The United States has two basic statutory tariff schedules: "normal trade relations" (NTR) tariffs that apply to WTO members and are generally low, and non-NTR tariffs that apply to nonmarket economies and are generally high—a vestige of the 1930 Smoot-Hawley Tariff Act. Prior to 2000, as a nonmarket economy that had not yet joined the WTO, China was in theory subject to non-NTR tariffs. In practice, however, these high tariffs were never applied; every year, as noted in the first chapter, the US Congress approved the lower applied tariffs on Chinese imports. Despite the fact that China never paid high tariffs, the requirement of an annual approval of lower tariffs by Congress exposed the country to a high degree of uncertainty. In October 2000, however, the US granted it with "permanent trade relations"— making the low tariff levels permanent and eliminating the uncertainty. Second, in 2001, China joined the WTO.

Between 2001 and 2004, US imports from China surged, and there was a rapid increase in offshoring by US firms. According to Pierce and Schott, these forces, which they labeled the "China shock" on the global economy, are largely responsible for the sudden and dramatic decline in US manufacturing employment during this period. Other economists have reached similar conclusions—notably in another seminal paper by David Autor, David Dorn, and Gordon Hanson, also in the *American Economic Review*, which referred to the shift as the "China syndrome."[20] (As a side note, these developments once again demonstrate the power of trade policy.)

Of course, the China shock is unlikely to have been the sole factor behind these developments in the United States, and many other advanced countries have experienced deindustrialization (i.e., the transition from manufacturing to services). Technology, automation in particular, has likely played an important role in the decline of manufacturing employment globally as workers are increasingly replaced by machines and robots. Nevertheless, the empirical strategies used in these papers (and others) credibly demonstrate that imports from China caused major disruption in the US labor market. Pierce and Schott show that industries that were more exposed to Chinese import competition fared worse than industries facing less competition, while Autor, Dorn, and Hanson—as discussed below—showed that local labor markets with a higher concentration of import-competing manufacturing industries fared worse than less exposed labor markets. Hence even if one does not fully accept the claim that the China shock was the main driver behind the decline of US manufacturing employment, it is clear that it changed the relative positions of workers employed in certain industries and/or living in certain regions. From the perspective of inequality, these relative effects matter just as much as, if not more than, the aggregate trends.

The effects of the China shock were most dramatically felt in the United States; Europe did not experience the same sharply negative shock. This is in part because many European countries normalized their trade relationships with China much earlier and in a much more gradual manner than the United States. Several European countries, such as Germany and Switzerland, also export to China as much as they import. These countries benefited from China's integration into the world trading system, as they saw their exports to China in key sectors (e.g., machinery and automobiles) increase.[21] In addition, many European countries have very different social protection systems and stronger social safety nets than the United States; this may have insulated European populations from the most adverse consequences of plant closures and unemployment. On the other hand, the China shock affected a great number of developing countries, which suddenly faced increased competition for their export industries—most notably in Latin America—but the specific detrimental effects on labor market inequality were most severe in the United States.

Regional Inequality The rapid and massive entry by China and other developing country exporters into the world trading system during the era of hyperglobalization was likely a contributing factor in manufacturing employment losses and wage stagnation in advanced economies. But more recent economic research including the paper by Autor, Dorn, and Hanson suggests a slightly refined, alternative interpretation, namely that trade's effects on labor market inequality is also largely a story about trade's effects on regional inequality. In short, the effects of global trade on a country's labor markets vary by region, based on the extent of each region's exposure to global trade.

While intuitive, this reflects an evolution in economic thinking beyond the aggregate effects of trade to a greater focus on its distributional consequences. As noted, Autor, Dorn, and Hanson's paper analyzes the effects of trade across local US labor markets—or "commuting zones" (CZs)—based on each CZ's exposure and vulnerability to competition from Chinese imports. Between 2000 and 2007, they found that CZs with higher concentrations of manufacturing industries and larger import penetration from China experienced sharper declines in manufacturing employment. Interestingly, the effects documented by Autor, Dorn, and Hanson led to a surprising conclusion: labor, it seemed, was not mobile across CZs. Prior to their study, most economists assumed that labor was highly mobile across local labor markets. Their finding thus raised an important question: What is the nature of mobility frictions that prevent workers affected by trade-related shocks from moving *within their own country* to pursue better job opportunities?

Typically, mobility constraints in the United States have been considered from the perspective of geographic frictions, including factors like the high rate of homeownership in the United States (compared to places like Europe, where more people rent). During an economic shock, owning a home can pose significant mobility challenges for workers who need or want to relocate. In addition to having to sell their home, they will likely need to do so at a discount if the local housing market is in a downturn, and they will likely need to repurchase a new home at a premium if they move to a region with more promising economic opportunities. Less well understood is how sectoral mobility may interact with and further constrain regional mobility. For example, if you are a laid-off auto worker in Detroit who wants to transition to the electronics or computer sector, in addition to having to acquire the necessary skills, you may need to move to the Bay Area or another technology hub to take advantage of local job opportunities, further exacerbating the mobility frictions.

The implications of Autor, Dorn, and Hanson's findings is that China alone was perhaps not solely responsible for the China syndrome; rather, local labor mobility frictions within the United States also played a role in producing the large effects. Exploring this distinct dimension of inequality, namely inequality across space, shifts the methodological focus for analyses of trade's effects on inequality. Similar findings were documented in the aforementioned study by Choi, Kuziemko, Washington, and Wright into the labor effects of NAFTA.[22] Employing a local labor markets approach similar to that of Autor, Dorn, and Hanson, their study documents large negative effects of NAFTA on US counties where employment depended on industries that were more vulnerable to the trade agreement's impacts. These results diverge from common wisdom at the time that trade had minimal labor market impacts in the United States before China's sharp trade expansion in the early 2000s.

Similar studies have found evidence of trade's effects on regional inequality within countries and the role of mobility frictions in developing countries. Importantly, many of these studies explore the effects of episodes of unilateral trade liberalization rather than import competition from China or any other country, and many focus on developing countries that were relatively unaffected by the China shock. Several of these developing country trade liberalization episodes have been explored in my earlier work, joint with Nina Pavcnik, the findings of which were summarized in the *Journal of Economic Literature*.[23] In particular, we explored how differential tariff changes in developing countries related to changing wage levels, skill premiums, and other dimensions of inequality in those countries. While we did find effects that were statistically significant, their magnitudes were small. In Latin

America, for example, we found that trade liberalization did affect labor markets, but it could not account for the substantial rise in inequality documented in several Latin American economies in the 1980s and 1990s. We did not, however, explore the dynamics of inequality across space identified by Autor, Dorn, and Hanson as well as Choi and colleagues. More recent work has found evidence of large effects of trade liberalization on regional inequality in developing countries (much larger than the effects on skill or wage premiums we had documented). Such findings offer further evidence that trade's large effects on labor markets in recent years, documented by many economists, are not only due to the emergence of China as a trade superpower, or to the rise of the skill premium, but rather highlight a different dimension of inequality: spatial inequality within countries, exacerbated by mobility frictions.

For instance, a 2010 paper by Petia Topalova measures the impact of trade liberalization on poverty and inequality following India's sharp trade liberalization in 1991.[24] Amid a balance-of-payments crisis in 1991, and as part of an International Monetary Fund structural adjustment program, the Indian government suddenly abandoned the extremely restrictive trade policies it had pursued since independence. Topolava uses the variation in industrial composition across Indian districts before liberalization as well as variation in the degree of liberalization across industries to analyze how the impacts of India's liberalization differed across the country. She finds that in rural districts concentrated with industries that were more exposed to liberalization, poverty reduction was slower during the 1990s by about 15 percent compared to the rest of India. Exploring the drivers of such large effects, Topalova finds that India's extremely limited labor mobility across regions and industries exacerbated the adverse impacts of liberalization. In regions where local labor laws inhibited workers' mobility the most, the poverty reduction was even lower.

Compounding the unequal effects of trade shocks across space, a 2017 paper by Rafael Dix-Carneiro and Brian Kovak using data from Brazil also shows how limited labor mobility within countries can exacerbate and prolong these adverse effects.[25] In the early 1990s, trade liberalization opened Brazil up to global markets and international competition. A convenient feature of the Brazilian trade liberalization is that—similar to India's liberalization, and in contrast to the China shock that unfolded gradually over two decades—it was implemented within a short time interval and completed by 1995. This allows one to trace its long-run impacts on local labor markets. Figure 2.8 shows the effects of this liberalization on Brazilian employment by comparing the regions hit hardest, namely manufacturing zones like São Paulo, with regions that were not affected. In the late 1980s, employment in the ultimately hard-hit regions was stable and slightly stronger, but following liberalization, employment sharply declined relative to the regions that were not affected.

On its own, this trend is not surprising: when an influx of imports triggers a negative demand shock, the standard economic models would expect labor markets affected by the shock to be more adversely affected in the short run. It is surprising, however, that these effects are so persistent and long-lasting. Standard economic models would predict labor markets to gradually recover as firms adjust and workers migrate to regions with better employment opportunities. What Dix-Carneiro and Kovak show is that there was no recovery in Brazil. In the regions hit hard by liberalization, employment keeps going down and then

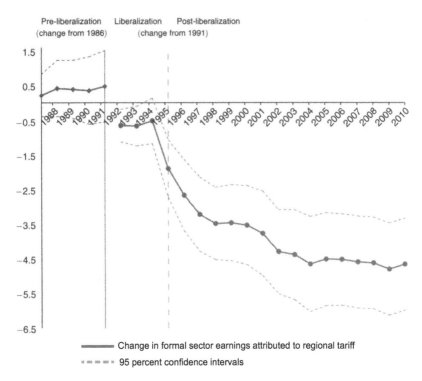

Figure 2.8
Effects of Brazilian trade liberalization on employment, 1988–2010. *Source:*
Rafael Dix-Carneiro and Brian Kovak, "Trade Liberalization and Regional
Dynamics," *American Economic Review* 107, no. 10 (October 2017):
2908–2946.

stays down at a significantly lower level for nearly twenty
years. Several studies on this topic have confirmed these
effects, which are often large, reflecting another recent shift
in economic thinking.

Figure 2.9 shows that a similar or even worse story
unfolded in terms of Brazilian workers' wages. In the late
1980s, worker earnings in the formal sector of regions ultimately hit hard by liberalization were increasing at a rapid

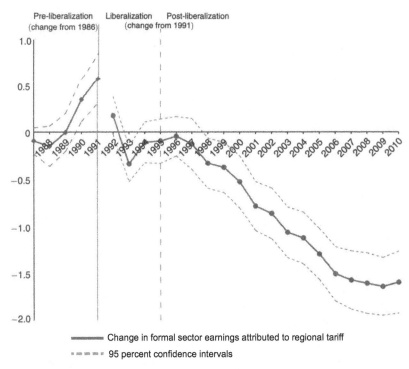

Figure 2.9
Effects of Brazilian trade liberalization on earnings, 1988–2010. *Source:*
Rafael Dix-Carneiro and Brian Kovak, "Trade Liberalization and Regional
Dynamics," *American Economic Review* 107, no. 10 (October 2017): 2908–
2946.

pace. After liberalization, wages fell sharply compared to
regions not affected by liberalization, and they continued
to decline for nearly two decades. The only reason earnings finally stabilized, as Dix-Carneiro and Kovak show,
is that workers left the formal sector and sought informal employment (i.e., businesses not registered by tax
authorities). But this is not a positive outcome; these jobs
are generally considered to be less desirable for workers,

with fewer benefits, less stability, and diminished job security. The transition to informality raises many questions about labor market frictions, which are explored in further work.[26] To the extent that these effects generalize to other contexts, they have profound implications for the relationship between trade and regional inequality.

Much research has also found that the adverse effects of trade can go well beyond labor markets. Autor, Dorn, and Hanson found that exposure to Chinese import shocks in US CZs also led to declining wages outside the manufacturing sector, steep drops in overall average household earnings, and rising overall transfer payments through federal and state income assistance programs (e.g., unemployment insurance, welfare payments, and other benefits). In India, studies by Eric Edmonds, Nina Pavcnik, and Petia Topalova found that regions that liberalized more experienced higher rates of child labor and less schooling (in relative terms), especially for girls, compared to regions that liberalized less.[27] In another study of Brazil, Dix-Carneiro and coauthors Rodrigo Soares and Gabriel Ulyssea found that import liberalization increased crime rates (again in relative terms) in the regions most impacted by import competition.[28]

Importantly, these are just relative effects; they do not suggest that entire economies were hurt by trade. Indeed, especially for developing countries, openness to trade is associated with many positive economic benefits. Nonetheless, there is a clear link between trade and regional inequality. Large regional disparities can be created when countries open up to trade—particularly through import liberalization, an approach frequently embraced during the last few decades, by developing and developed countries alike. Again, effects so large and persistent are surprising; standard economic models would expect employment, wages, and nonlabor market effects to recover as people move to find better opportunities, at least in the long run. But this evidence suggests that workers do not move much following trade shocks in the short or long run—nearly a decade in the case of Autor, Dorn, and Hanson's research, and twenty years in Dix-Carneiro and Kovak's study—leading to significant costs that magnify over time.

This is a major new insight in economics, and it is particularly surprising in light of recent policy debates about immigration. In advanced economies, many policy makers are increasingly concerned that too many low-skilled, low-income workers from developing countries are migrating into their labor markets. These concerns stem, more or less, from a view that there is *too much* mobility in the global economy. The latest economics research suggests, by contrast, that a major problem—within countries at least, in both developed and developing countries—is *too little* mobility across space, producing large and persistent effects on regional inequality following trade shocks.

2.3.2 The Unequal Effects on Consumers

The other dimension of inequality within countries is related to the consumer channel. In general, we would expect consumers to benefit from a higher degree of international integration through lower prices. In standard economic models, reducing trade barriers reduces consumer prices in two ways: by lowering production costs for domestic firms due to the availability of cheaper foreign-made "intermediate inputs," which can also drive down the prices of domestic inputs, as long as these cost reductions get passed on to consumers in the form of lower prices; and/or by increasing competition for domestic firms due to the presence of cheaper imported "finished goods." Consumers can also benefit from trade by gaining access to a higher quality and greater variety of products. This thinking makes intuitive sense, is well supported by much theoretical work in the economics literature, and has long served as a rationale for trade economists and policy makers to advocate for more free trade. But do the data support it? Surprisingly, there is not a wealth of direct evidence for how trade affects prices, and there has been relatively limited empirical work on the consumer side of globalization. The evidence that does exist, however—much of which comes from developing countries—is somewhat mixed.

Recent evidence from India, for example, suggests that the standard economic theories about consumer gains from trade do not always play out in practice—especially when markets are not fully competitive. In 2016, for instance, I coauthored a paper with Jan De Loecker, Amit Khandelwal, and Nina Pavcnik that analyzed production data from Indian firms between 1989 and 2003, spanning the periods before and after India's trade liberalization—the same period analyzed in Topalova's study of trade's unequal effects on workers that was highlighted above.[29] Utilizing firm data on prices and quantities, we developed a framework for understanding how opening up to global trade affected Indian firms' marginal production costs, the prices paid by Indian consumers, and firm profits—as reflected in the price markups placed by firms on finished products.

Figure 2.10 shows the main findings from our analysis. We found that India's trade liberalization—during which output tariff levels declined by 62 percentage points on average, including sharp tariff reductions on both intermediate inputs and finished goods—reduced firms' marginal costs by an average of 31 percent, primarily due to the availability of cheaper foreign inputs. While consumer prices also declined, they did so only by 18 percent on average—much less than most trade models would predict. Why didn't firms pass their lower production costs on to consumers in the form of lower prices? The answer, we found, was that firms captured most of this value for themselves: the average Indian firm profits (in the form of price markups) actually *increased* by about 13 percent after liberalization. This runs counter to standard economic theory, which would expect trade liberalization to increase competition and narrow domestic firms' profit margins, as they now must compete with cheaper foreign imports. So what explains our result? Counterfactual analyses of trade policies used to assess the effects of liberalization episodes on consumers typically assume either perfect competition or constant price markups. In contrast, our study provides evidence that price markups can vary in ways that are strongly affected by trade policy.

Of course, these results do not necessarily capture the total welfare benefits to Indian consumers from trade liberalization. Indeed, product quality also increased, and there was even a link between market power and product variety and innovation: firms that enjoyed the highest price markup increases were also the most likely to introduce new products—likely because they used higher profits to invest in innovation and new technologies. Nonetheless, India's experience shows that the gains from trade often do not pass through an economy equally. While Indian firms and consumers both benefited from the government's trade liberalization in the 1990s, firms captured more of the benefits—at least in the short and medium run.[30] The reason is that many firms, instead of passing the cost reductions they experienced from tariff reductions on to their customers in the form of lower prices on a one-for-one basis, chose to increase their profit margins. As a result, the average prices facing consumers did decline, but not by as

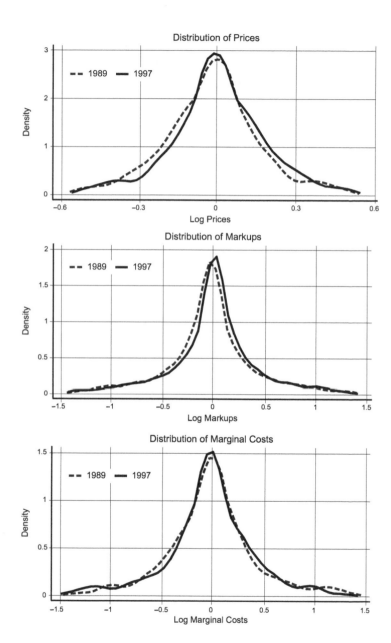

much as the average cost declines enjoyed by firms. This phenomenon could well have implications for inequality within India and for the distributional effects of trade in any country. Specifically, it suggests that trade may have contributed to the increase of yet another dimension of inequality: inequality between consumers and producers.

Several other studies have documented the rise in markups and firm profits around the world in recent decades. A recent paper by Jan De Loecker, Jan Eeckhout, and Gabriel Unger, for example, documents the evolution of market power in the US economy since the 1950s by analyzing firm-level data to estimate the aggregate price markups.[31] Figure 2.11 shows their striking results: while the aggregate markups were more or less stable between 1955 and 1980, they rose steadily thereafter from 21 percent (above marginal cost) to 61 percent in 2016. During the same period, the average profit rate increased from 1 to 8 percent. Critically, De Loecker, Eeckhout, and Unger also found that markups did not increase proportionally across all firms. Rather, a few large firms enjoyed higher markups, but the majority of firms saw no increase in markups and lost market share—suggesting a reallocation of market power. This reflects the rise of the so-called "superstar" firm in the United States and other advanced economies in recent decades, as many industries have become increasingly

---

Figure 2.10
Effects of Indian trade liberalization on marginal production costs, consumer prices, and firm profits. *Notes:* The sample only includes firm-product pairs present in 1989 and 1997. Outliers above and below the thirty-fourth and ninety-seventh percentiles are trimmed. *Source:* Jan De Loecker, Pinelopi Goldberg, Amit Khandelwal, and Nina Pavcnik, "Prices, Markups and Trade Reform," *Econometrica* 84, no. 2 (March 2016): 445–510.

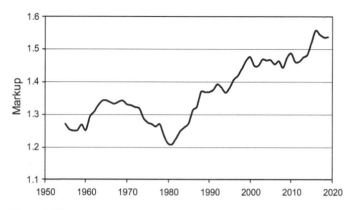

Figure 2.11
Rise in US markups, 1950–2020. *Source:* Jan De Loecker, Jan Eeckhout, and
Gabriel Unger, "The Rise of Market Power and the Macroeconomic Impli-
cations," *Quarterly Journal of Economics* 135, no. 2 (May 2020): 561–644.

concentrated, with a small number of productive firms
accounting for large shares of the market and large profits.

These trends are not limited to the United States. In
a follow-up working paper, De Loecker and Eeckhout
reproduce the same analysis for the global economy. Utilizing four decades of data from the financial statements
of more than 70,000 firms in 134 countries, De Loecker
and Eeckhout document that the aggregate global markup
increased from 1.15 percent in 1980 to around 1.6 percent
in 2016.[32] Figure 2.12 shows their findings at the continent
level: while markups rose the most in North America and
Europe, and the least in Africa and the emerging economies
in Latin America—two regions of the world that happen
to be much less integrated into global trade networks—the
overall trends are remarkably consistent across regions.
As with the US analysis, these changes highlight a redistribution of value toward large firms (though De Loecker
and Eeckhout do find that this phenomenon varies

considerably by region). Notably, increasing firm profits are associated with declining shares of income accruing to labor—a trend seen in both advanced and developing economies—suggesting another reallocation of economic power. Just as firms have captured a higher share of the gains from trade and technology, rather than pass those benefits on to consumers, they have also failed to pass the benefits on to workers.

To what extent did globalization contribute to the widespread rise in firm profits? After all, these seismic shifts in the global economy unfolded during an era of historic trade growth. Unfortunately, this question is difficult to answer with much certainty. In some specific cases, it is clear that global trade has affected market power and contributed to higher inequality between consumers and producers; as our India analysis showed, the trade liberalization in 1991 had direct impacts on outsized firm profits for the remainder of the decade. But in other contexts, or at the global level, such causal links are more challenging to identify. There is, however, plenty of strongly suggestive evidence.

The World Bank's 2020 *World Development Report*, for instance, explored these issues in the context of GVC expansion—finding a wealth of evidence that the gains from GVC participation were not distributed equally within countries between consumers and producers. Figure 2.13 shows the correlations between firm markups and GVC participation in the textile sectors of Belgium, France, Germany, Great Britain, Japan, and the United States over three decades. For each country, the gray line indicates the aggregate markups (or average firm profits) in the textile sector and the black line indicates GVC integration. While not causal, there is clearly a relationship between the growth of GVC activity and the rise in markups—and

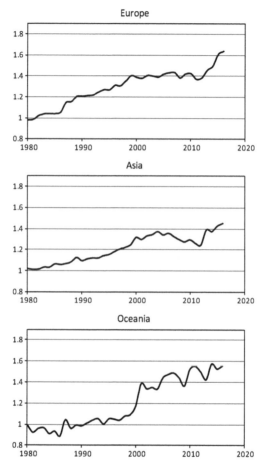

Figure 2.12
Rise in global markups, 1980–2016. *Source:* Jan De Loecker and Jan Eeck-hout, "Global Market Power" (NBER Working Paper 24768, National Bureau of Economic Research, Cambridge, MA, June 2018), https://www.nber.org/papers/w24768.

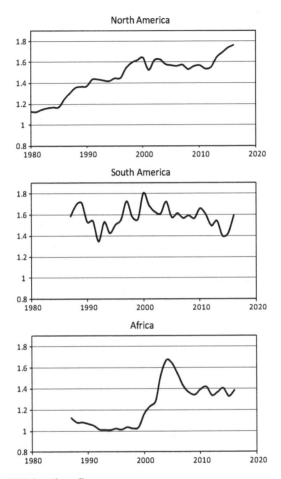

Figure 2.12 (continued)

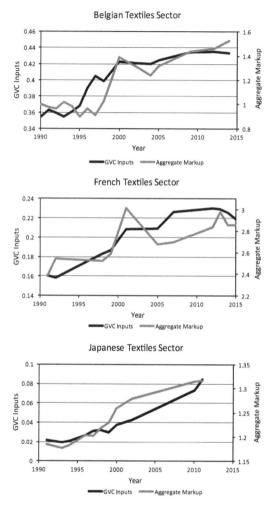

Figure 2.13
Firm markups and GVC participation in various textiles sectors. *Note:*
The left y-axis measures the share of foreign value added in the gross
exports of each country's textile sector. The right y-axis measures the
share-weighted average markup of listed companies in the textile sector.
The markups are calculated following Jan De Loecker and Jan Eeckhout,

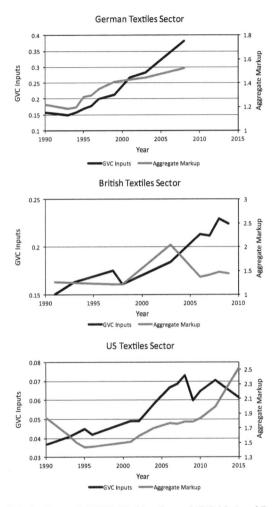

"Global Market Power" (NBER Working Paper 24768, National Bureau of Economic Research, Cambridge, MA, June 2018), https://www.nber.org /papers/w24768. *Source:* World Bank staff, unpublished analysis for World Bank, *World Development Report 2020: Trading for Development in the Age of Global Value Chains* (Washington, DC: World Bank, 2019), using data from Eora and Worldscope.

these trends are consistent for most advanced countries in the textiles industry. A major driver of these shifts in textiles is the highly competitive retail clothing industry, which in recent decades has increasingly moved its production centers from advanced economies to developing countries—allowing firms to reduce consumer prices while also increasing profits. To cite just one well-documented example, Everlane, a California company committed to transparent pricing, reports the cost breakdown and average prices of all of its products, and according to the company's website, a pair of jeans that customarily sells for $170 is produced for only $34.

In light of the aforementioned evidence from India and the United States as well as the global trends on market power, these dynamics should not be surprising. Firms that participate in GVCs can expect to benefit from lower costs of inputs; unconstrained by domestic supply, they can realize increased growth and productivity through economies of scale, especially in mass production manufacturing; and these advantages disproportionately accrue to larger firms, which can afford the fixed costs of exporting, importing, and scaling. GVCs thus contribute to the emergence of huge, multinational "superstar" firms that enjoy outsized market power, large profit margins, and disproportionate bargaining power over their suppliers. Firms participating in GVCs typically pass a smaller share of the realized cost savings on to their consumers (in the form of lower prices) as well as a smaller share of their higher profit margins on to workers (in the form of higher wages). As a side note, GVCs also contribute to other dimensions of inequality, beyond the inequality between producers and consumers that is the focus of this section. For example, women are generally employed in lower-value-added segments, and women owners and managers are largely missing in

GVCs. The inequality effects of GVCs have a geographic dimension too, with GVCs concentrated in urban agglomerations and in border regions for countries neighboring GVC partners.

It is important to note that GVCs affect developing countries as well—often in opposite ways. The trend in figure 2.13 underscores the benefits of "backward" GVC participation, as advanced economies have transferred large parts of their production to developing countries.[33] What are the effects of "forward" GVC participation in developing countries? Figure 2.14 compares US textile sector trends with those of India. It is clear that India has experienced an opposite trend than the United States in recent years, with a negative relationship between markups and GVC participation. The short-run effects we saw in India immediately following its trade policy reforms—as Indian firms with Indian market power increased profits at the expense of Indian consumers—seem to have subsequently been overshadowed in the long run by larger global trends. The 2020 *World Development Report* identified similar negative relationships for ten other developing countries in the textile and apparel sector, controlling for country-fixed effects. (Notably, in China the relationship between markups and GVC participation has been positive, similar to advanced economies.) As large multinational firms from advanced economies have seen higher profits, the domestic firms in developing countries that sell them inputs have gotten squeezed.

Of course, this is not to suggest that globalization is solely responsible for all of these trends. While the evidence from textiles is particularly suggestive—given that this industry has been fundamentally reshaped by GVCs—the picture in other sectors is somewhat more mixed. Figure 2.15, for example, conducts the same analysis for the

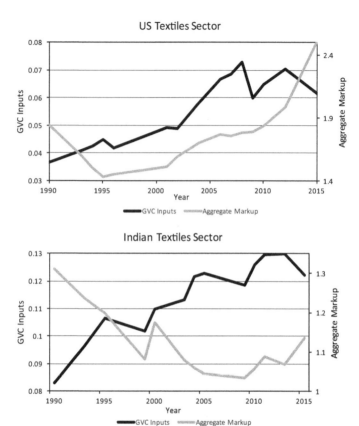

Figure 2.14
Firm markups and GVC participation in the US and Indian textiles sectors. *Note:* The left y-axis in the top panel measures the share of foreign value added in the gross exports of the US textile sector (backward GVC participation). The left y-axis in the bottom panel measures the share of domestic value added in India embodied in importing countries' exports to third countries (forward GVC participation). The right y-axis in both panels measures the share-weighted average markup of listed companies in the textile sector. The markups are calculated following Jan De Loecker and Jan Eeckhout, "Global Market Power" (NBER Working Paper 24768, National Bureau of Economic Research, Cambridge, MA, June 2018), https://www.nber.org/papers/w24768. Similar results hold across countries and sectors. *Sources:* World Bank, *World Development Report 2020: Trading for Development in the Age of Global Value Chains* (Washington, DC: World Bank, 2019), 85, using data from Eora and Worldscope.

same countries as in figure 2.14, but for the transport sector. Despite having become highly integrated with GVCs in recent decades, these countries' transport industries have not seen markups rise at the same pace or magnitude as in textiles. Globalization is clearly an important part of the story about rising inequality between consumers and producers within countries over recent decades, however the narrative does not uniformly apply to all sectors in all countries.

Looking ahead, it will be interesting to see how new technologies affect GVC participation by firms in different countries and the resulting effects on inequality—most plausibly through the worker channel rather than the consumer channel. Automation, robotics, 3D printing, and artificial intelligence could present challenges for developing countries that have so far benefited from GVC participation due to their abundance of low-cost workers. One specific concern is that companies from advanced economies will "reshore" or return production operations to their home countries, constraining developing countries' prospects for export-led industrialization. Thus far, however, the emerging evidence is fairly encouraging.[34] Automation has so far increased trade with developing countries rather than reducing it, though the effects vary across countries and sectors. One manifestation is that many of the robots currently being adopted by advanced-economy firms are manufactured in developing countries due to their lower costs for parts and labor. In the more distant future, however, automation by manufacturing firms in developing countries could significantly undermine labor and pose certain challenges to these countries' long-run growth and development prospects. Once all countries adopt robots, there will be little incentive to take advantage of lower labor costs in developing countries through trade

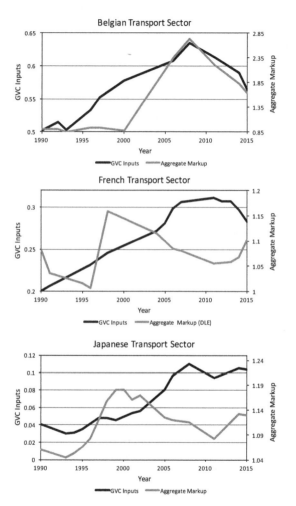

Figure 2.15
Firm markups and GVC participation in various transport sectors. *Note:*
The left y-axis measures the share of foreign value added in the gross
exports of each country's transport sector. The right y-axis measures the
share-weighted average markup of listed companies in the transport
sector. The markups are calculated following Jan De Loecker and Jan

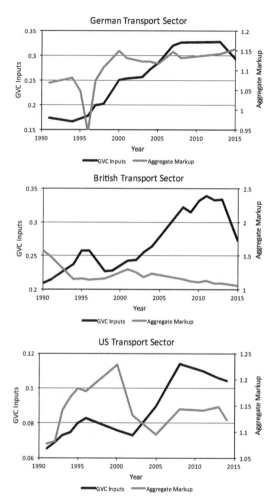

Eeckhout, "Global Market Power" (NBER Working Paper 24768, National Bureau of Economic Research, Cambridge, MA, June 2018), https://www.nber.org/papers/w24768. *Sources:* World Bank staff, unpublished analysis for World Bank, *World Development Report 2020: Trading for Development in the Age of Global Value Chains* (Washington, DC: World Bank, 2019), using data from Eora and Worldscope.

and foreign direct investment. As such, increased automation in both developed and developing countries is likely to have very unequal effects between and within countries, further increasing skill premiums and profits while shifting resources from workers and/or consumers to firms.

Returning to trade's unequal effects on consumers, our discussion thus far has highlighted that price reductions brought about by trade, while beneficial to consumers, may still exacerbate certain dimensions of inequality, namely inequality between producers and consumers. As we have seen, this can occur when the consumer price reductions are not as large as the production cost reductions brought about by trade, such that firm profit margins increase as a result. But there is another dimension of trade's unequal effects on consumers, namely *inequality among consumers*. In other words, how are the consumer gains from trade distributed among consumers, especially across different income levels? Does trade benefit low-income consumers more than high-income consumers, thus contributing to a decline in inequality—or does the opposite occur? Once again, the existing evidence on these questions is mixed and inconclusive.

On the one hand, globalization is perhaps the best method for quickly increasing the availability of new products and offering them at lower prices to poor consumers. In Mexico, for example, a recent analysis of microlevel household data by David Atkin, Benjamin Faber, and Marco Gonzalez-Navarro found that the entry of foreign supermarkets causes large welfare gains for the average household, predominantly driven by a reduction in the cost of living—both through direct consumer gains from the foreign stores and increased product variety as well as price reductions at domestic stores due to foreign competition.[35] While the researchers found these gains to be positive on average for all income groups, the benefits, however, were higher for wealthy consumers; this could be because many foreign stores target wealthier demographics or because very poor consumers lack physical access to some large foreign retail stores like Walmart, which are designed for shoppers with cars. Based on these results, one would conclude that globalization in Mexico—while benefiting consumers substantially—ultimately contributed to an increase in consumer inequality by making wealthier consumers better off.

Another recent paper by Xavier Jaravel and Erick Sager found that US consumer prices fell substantially in recent decades due to increased trade with China.[36] Analyzing comprehensive price microdata back to 1988, Jaravel and Sager estimate that a 1 percentage point increase in import penetration from China led to a decline in US consumer prices by 1 to 2 percent (depending on the specification), and that these price declines were predominantly driven by declining firm markups for goods produced in the United States. These estimates imply that for every US job displaced, trade with China increased US consumer surplus by about $400,000. New work by David Dorn and Peter Levell using data from the United Kingdom reports similar results, implying large gains for the average British consumer as a result of the China shock.[37] They found, however, that the gains were equally distributed among consumers across the income spectrum, suggesting that trade with China, while benefiting the average consumer, did not reduce consumer inequality—certainly not to the extent needed to compensate for the adverse impacts on labor markets. Another recent paper by Kirill Borusyak and Xavier Jaravel, focusing on US data, reports similar findings. The general message of this work is that trade with China was beneficial for the *average* consumer in advanced countries as prices declined by more than average nominal wages. The net gains from trade with China were unequally distributed, however, since the benefits from price declines were spread evenly across the population while the adverse labor market effects hit certain regions harder—ultimately contributing to increased inequality.[38]

In general, what matters for inequality is not the size of price reductions caused by trade but rather their incidence across income groups, which depends on those groups' spending habits. A priori, we can expect trade to benefit poorer consumers more, as the poor tend to spend a relatively larger share of their income on tradable goods—a point elaborated in a 2016 paper by Pablo Fajgelbaum and Amit Khandelwal.[39] The rich, however, spend relatively more on import-intensive tradable goods such as electronics and relatively less on goods with small import shares such as food. As a result, the effects of trade on consumer inequality depend on which of these two effects dominates. The aforementioned analyses by Dorn and Levell as well as Borusyak and Jaravel show that at least for the case of Chinese import competition in the United Kingdom and the United States, the two channels approximately cancel each other out so that the net effect of trade on consumer inequality is zero.

This conclusion seems to contrast with the commonly held view in recent years that trade, especially with China, has disproportionately benefited low-income consumers in advanced economies—what many have called the "Walmart effect," as Walmart and similar stores sell many low-price products imported from China that are particularly appealing to low-income households. What explains such a widely held view, if the evidence doesn't support it? While there are many potential answers, data limitations may play an important role. David Atkin's comment for the

Deaton Review, for instance, notes the many measurement and identification difficulties associated with assessing trade's impact on prices.[40] Chief among these difficulties is the lack of the highly disaggregated price data needed to assess price impacts across the income distribution. While expenditure surveys provide economists with large data sets to analyze price effects, they record expenditures and quantities at a very coarse level, making it difficult to capture differences in the specific brands consumed by the rich or the poor. (Needless to say, for example, a price reduction on imported Armani jackets from Italy would have very different inequality implications than a price reduction on imported jackets from Ethiopia.) Retail scanner data, such as those provided by Nielsen, collect real-time price and other information that can partly compensate for this lack of granularity. Such data, however, often do not include major product categories that benefit substantially from trade, such as automobiles. Furthermore, such data have become available only recently, often making the samples derived from them too short for credible empirical analysis. All of these difficulties may contribute to the view that trade's price effects disproportionately benefit the poor.

Likewise, existing price studies fail to capture that most people in most countries, including the global poor, now have access to a range of incredible goods and services, including smartphones and internet access, which would have been unthinkable a few decades ago. The two key factors that made this possible are technological development and international trade, namely through cost and price reductions made possible by international specialization within GVCs. In earlier times, the notional price of such goods and services was essentially infinity for the many lower-income households that could not afford them. Thanks to trade and technology, this price has declined to a finite number that many low-income consumers can afford. While hard to formally measure, the impact of such changes may very well be a first-order concern for the well-being of millions or billions of poor households around the world. The challenge of measuring such transformational shifts is perhaps the most important shortcoming of efforts to analyze the effects of trade on consumer inequality.

To conclude, the effects of globalization on prices and consumers are much the same as its effects on workers and firms: as with so much about globalization, the effects on inequality are complex, difficult to untangle, and subject to a high degree of interaction with factors that are constantly in flux (e.g., technology).

3   Conclusion

The effects of globalization are both unequal and highly uneven. They are uneven between countries and within countries; they are uneven across regions and demographics; and they are uneven between producers, consumers, and workers. There is ample evidence that globalization exacerbates some dimensions of inequality, just as there is ample evidence that globalization reduces other dimensions of inequality (most important, global inequality). The underlying challenge is that inequality is a deeply broad concept. In many ways, the effects of globalization on inequality depend entirely on what dimension of inequality you are focused on.

The ideal research and policy response to such a challenging state of affairs would be to identify, harness, and leverage globalization's positive features while preventing, mitigating, or compensating for its negative effects. Unfortunately, researchers' understanding of all the evidence and policy makers' ability to act on it are many years from this ideal scenario. Perhaps only one broad finding is certain and clear as of yet: globalization causes disruption, which often requires significant transition and adjustment. Indeed, much of the recent backlash has been focused on these complications from trade rather than on any abstract notions about it. Yet standard economic models of international trade, like much of the policy debates about it, tend to focus on the steady-state end results, be they gains or losses. At the very least, a key takeaway from this monograph and the evidence it showcases is that globalization is a process, not an end state. A major implication of this takeaway is that researchers and policy makers should focus much more seriously on the disruptions, transitions, and adjustments from globalization than on estimating, defending, or condemning its ultimate impacts.

Such a focus has at least three additional implications. The first is that spatial or regional inequality is one of the most significant effects of globalization and should be a major priority for researchers and policy makers going forward. Regional inequality is significant not only because the empirical evidence increasingly suggests that globalization's adverse effects are quite spatially isolated but also because it has emerged as an important driver of the recent backlash against globalization. As such, while the unequal effects of globalization are many, regional inequality is perhaps the most likely to have significant social and political consequences. This provides potential justification for greater focus on and experimentation with so-called place-based policies. While the field of economics has traditionally had a negative view of place-based policies, due to their potentially distortionary effects, they certainly merit reconsideration as a tool for addressing regional inequality. For example, efforts to support displaced workers could be regionally targeted. There is growing evidence that retraining or "upskilling" programs are often ineffective, but such programs and other efforts—including policies for workforce development, social protection, and job creation—might be more promising if they focused on the *places* that need them most.

Second, the dramatic growth of firm profits in light of globalization demands greater focus and policy action. The emergence of GVCs, growth of global technology platforms, and reallocation of capital and market power toward incredibly large, highly mobile, and deeply connected "superstar" firms all raise important questions about the relationships between firms, government, and society. While these questions are timeless and fundamental, their contemporary manifestations are highly novel and—technically, legally, and politically—almost endlessly complex. First and foremost, addressing the recent increase in firm markups demands greater attention to how these large global firms are taxed and regulated.

Finally and crucially, the issues raised in this monograph underscore the vital importance of greater international cooperation—on trade, but also in many other economic arenas. As noted, many of the unequal effects of globalization go beyond the realm of trade while having important implications for it. Likewise, much of the increased trade frictions seen in recent years were not only due to narrowly defined trade policies like tariffs; rather, they involved "behind-the-border" measures, nontariff trade restrictions, and other aspects of economic activity that affect trade or inequality but are much harder to measure.

The recent tensions and backlash against globalization pose formidable challenges for the global trading system, but there are still significant opportunities for greater international cooperation. Regional trade, for example, offers tremendous promise—on its own, but also as a counterbalance to rising global uncertainty. While the European Union represents a somewhat controversial model these days (given Brexit, its negative monetary outcomes, and other challenges), there is little doubt that establishing a free trade zone in Europe generated highly positive outcomes for many European countries as well as for many workers and consumers across the income spectrum. Around the world, from Africa and the Middle East to South America and Southeast Asia, there are many regional and subregional markets with large populations that have not yet achieved a high degree of regional interconnection. Many of the countries in these regions have already liberalized and harmonized their trade policies to join the WTO and participate in GVCs; increasing intraregional trade between them is a distinct area of opportunity. Hence even as multilateralism wanes, and new geopolitical concerns and alliances emerge, it is likely that globalization will continue while taking on a different face: GVCs may partially or entirely relocate their operations to different parts of the world, for example, and regionalism may become the new form of globalization.

Along these lines, the potential for surprising shifts in global trade arrangements are reflected in my aforementioned paper with coauthors showing how the US-China trade war created new trade opportunities for several "bystander countries."[1] As noted, these countries increased their exports to the United States (which was to be expected, since US imports from China were reallocated to other exporters), but also to the rest of the world, *increasing* their world exports amid the trade war. Notably, the countries that benefited the most had deep existing trade agreements and high stocks of foreign direct investment—in other words, countries already well integrated into the global trading system. In a different paper, Pol Antras explores the prospects for "reshoring," or efforts by multinational firms to move their manufacturing activities back to the home country of their headquarters.[2] Antras argues that the fixed costs incurred by firms to establish their operations across the world are large and sunk by nature, creating disincentives to reshore unless faced with negative shocks of considerable magnitude. Despite tough trade rhetoric in recent years and the worrisome outlook for globalization, we do not seem to have reached that point yet. Notwithstanding the possibility of major new policy developments, these arguments suggest that globalization may go on despite continued trade tensions and flagging multilateralism, albeit in a different and more subdued form.

One area where greater multilateral cooperation is essential, however, is the global effort to address climate change. The effects of climate change are expected to be complex and highly unequal, while the challenges of mitigating or adapting to them will be formidable. Several of the tensions in the arena of global trade are relevant to the climate issue, including conflicts between countries. For instance, there is significant tension in the climate arena between advanced countries—which are predominantly responsible for the bulk of historic carbon emissions, and which have achieved such high levels of affluence that they can afford to refocus their economies toward lower- or slower-growth strategies that prioritize environmental sustainability—and developing countries, especially low-income countries and those affected by war or deprivation, which are eager to accelerate economic growth and development. These countries understandably do not wish their future growth, development, and escape from poverty to be constrained by global efforts on problems they did not create. In this case, regionalism does not offer a way out of the difficulties associated with negotiating and resolving these tensions between countries. Emissions do not understand borders, regions, or continents; the very nature of the problem calls for global measures to address it, and such measures require multilateral agreements.

In many ways, the outlook for international agreement on climate is far more difficult than it is for issues like globalization—and as we have learned amid the COVID-19 pandemic, war in Ukraine, and risks of a global slowdown, other global challenges will surely arise that are similarly vexing and disruptive. Yet as this monograph has shown, the evolution of globalization, its unequal effects between and within countries, and public attitudes and policies toward or against it have been anything but straightforward. With climate change, pandemics, and other challenges as yet unknown, we should likewise expect them to unfold in complex and unpredictable ways. As such, enhancing our response to the unequal effects of globalization today—by tackling regional inequalities, addressing the growth of firm profits, and strengthening multilateral cooperation on all dimensions of trade—will help prepare the global community to respond to the challenges of tomorrow.

Notes

Preface

1. IFS Deaton Review of Inequalities, Institute for Fiscal Studies, accessed February 28, 2022, https://ifs.org.uk/inequality.

2. For a closely related study of this theme that specifically revolves around the effects of globalization on within-country inequality, see David Dorn and Peter Levell, "Trade and Inequality in Europe and the United States," IFS Deaton Review of Inequalities, Institute for Fiscal Studies, accessed February 28, 2022, https://ifs.org.uk/inequality/trade-and-inequality-in-europe-and-the-us.

Chapter 1

1. For consistency, figure 1.3 includes data only up to 2014 because the original data source—Michel Fouquin and Jules Hugot, "Two Centuries of Bilateral Trade and Gravity Data: 1827–2014" (CEPII Working Paper No. 2016–14, May 2016), http://www.cepii.fr/pdf_pub/wp/2016/wp2016-14.pdf—does not include disaggregated data for later years. Figure 1.2, by contrast, extends the sample up to 2019 by merging data from two sources: Fouquin and Hugot, "Two Centuries of Bilateral Trade and Gravity Data"; World Bank database. As evident from figure 1.2, there was no major trend reversal post-2014.

2. Nina Pavcnik, "The Impact of Trade on Inequality in Developing Countries," *Jackson Hole Economic Policy Symposium Proceedings* (Kansas City: Federal Reserve Bank of Kansas City, August 2017), 61–114.

3. For a detailed discussion, see Pinelopi Goldberg and Nina Pavcnik, "The Effects of Trade Policy," in *Handbook of Commercial Policy (Volume*

1, Part A), ed. Kyle Bagwell and Robert Staiger (Amsterdam: Elsevier, 2016), 161–206.

4. Roger Altman and Richard Haass, "Why the Trans-Pacific Partnership Matters," New York Times, April 3, 2015, https://www.nytimes.com/2015/04/04/opinion/why-the-trans-pacific-partnership-matters.html. Emphasis added.

5. Paul Krugman, "Growing World Trade: Causes and Consequences," Brookings Papers on Economic Activity 1 (1995): 328.

6. Lant Pritchett, "Immigration: Ending Global Apartheid," interview by Kerry Howley, Reason, February 2008, https://reason.com/2008/01/24/ending-global-apartheid.

7. For a review of this early evidence, see Alan Deardorff and Robert Stern, The Michigan Model of World Production and Trade: Theory and Applications (Cambridge, MA: MIT Press, 1985).

8. Andrew Rose, "Do We Really Know That the WTO Increases Trade?," American Economic Review 94, no. 1 (March 2004): 98–114.

9. Kei-Mu Yi, "Can Vertical Specialization Explain the Growth of World Trade?," Journal of Political Economy 111, no. 1 (February 2003): 52–102.

10. My longtime coauthor Nina Pavcnik and I have written extensively on this topic. See, for example, Goldberg and Pavcnik, "The Effects of Trade Policy."

11. For a discussion of the effects of TRIPS on developing countries, see Pinelopi Goldberg, "Intellectual Property Rights Protection in Developing Countries: The Case of Pharmaceuticals," Journal of the European Economic Association 8, no. 2–3 (May 2010): 326–353; Shubham Chaudhuri, Pinelopi Goldberg, and Panle Jia, "Estimating the Effects of Global Patent Protection in Pharmaceuticals: A Case Study of Quinolones in India," American Economic Review 96, no. 5 (December 2006): 1477–1514.

12. For estimates, see Pablo Fajgelbaum, Pinelopi Goldberg, Patrick Kennedy, and Amit Khandelwal, "The Return to Protectionism," Quarterly Journal of Economics 135, no. 1 (February 2020): 1–55.

13. Claudia Hofmann, Alberto Osnago, and Michele Ruta, "Horizontal Depth: A New Database on the Content of Preferential Trade Agreements" (Policy Research Working Paper No. 7981, World Bank, Washington, DC, February 2017), https://openknowledge.worldbank.org/handle/10986/26148.

14. A recent paper estimates that 54 percent of all protectionist interventions were nontariff barriers in 2010, and that this percentage had reached

61 percent by 2016. See Luisa Kinzius, Alexander Sandkamp, and Erdal Yalcin, "Trade Protection and the Role of Non-Tariff Barriers," *Review of World Economics* 155, no. 4 (November 2019): 603–643.

15. Fajgelbaum, Goldberg, Kennedy, and Khandelwal, "The Return to Protectionism."

16. Costas Arkolakis, Arnaud Costinot, and Andres Rodríguez-Clare, "New Trade Models, Same Old Gains?," *American Economic Review* 102, no. 1 (February 2012): 94–130.

17. Pablo Fajgelbaum, Pinelopi Goldberg, Patrick Kennedy, Amit Khandelwal, and Daria Taglioni, "The US-China Trade War and Global Reallocations" (NBER Working Paper No. 29562, National Bureau of Economic Research, Cambridge, MA, December 2021), https://www.nber.org/papers/w29562.

18. Pinelopi Goldberg and Tristan Reed, "Income Distribution, International Integration and Sustained Poverty Reduction" (Policy Research Working Paper No. 9342, World Bank, Washington, DC, July 2020), https://openknowledge.worldbank.org/handle/10986/34260.

Chapter 2

1. Anna Maria Mayda and Dani Rodrik, "Why Are Some People (and Countries) More Protectionist than Others?," *European Economic Review* 49, no. 6 (August 2005): 1393–1430.

2. Esteban Méndez-Chacón and Diana van Patten, "Voting on a Trade Agreement: Firm Networks and Attitudes toward Openness" (NBER Working Paper No. 30058, National Bureau of Economic Research, Cambridge, MA, May 2022), https://www.nber.org/papers/w30058.

3. Jiwon Choi, Ilyana Kuziemko, Ebonya Washington, and Gavin Wright, "Local Employment and Political Effects of Trade Deals: Evidence from NAFTA" (NBER Working Paper No. 29525, National Bureau of Economic Research, Cambridge, MA, November 2021), https://www.nber.org/papers/w29525.

4. Yi Che, Yi Lu, Justin Pierce, Peter Schott, and Zhigang Tao, "Does Trade Liberalization with China Influence US Elections?" (NBER Working Paper No. 22178, National Bureau of Economic Research, Cambridge, MA, April 2016), https://www.nber.org/papers/w22178; David Autor, David Dorn, Gordon Hanson, and Kaveh Majlesi, "Importing Political Polarization? The Electoral Consequences of Rising Trade Exposure," *American Economic Review* 110, no. 10 (October 2020): 3139–3183.

5. Clément Malgouyres, "Trade Shocks and Far-Right Voting: Evidence from French Presidential Elections" (Robert Schuman Centre for Advanced Studies Research Paper No. RSCAS 2017/21, Florence, Italy, March 2017); Christian Dippel, Robert Gold, and Stephan Heblich, "Globalization and Its (Dis-)Content: Trade Shocks and Voting Behavior" (NBER Working Paper No. 21812, National Bureau of Economic Research, Cambridge, MA, December 2015), https://www.nber.org/papers/w21812.

6. Italo Colantone and Piero Stanig, "Global Competition and Brexit," *American Political Science Review* 112, no. 2 (May 2018): 201–218.

7. Angus Deaton, *The Great Escape: Health, Wealth, and the Origins of Inequality* (Princeton, NJ: Princeton University Press, 2013).

8. Branko Milanovic, *Global Inequality: A New Approach for the Age of Globalization* (Cambridge, MA: Harvard University Press, 2016).

9. World Bank, *World Development Report 2006: Equity and Development* (Washington, DC: World Bank, 2006).

10. Christoph Lakner and Branko Milanovic, "Global Income Distribution: From the Fall of the Berlin Wall to the Great Recession," *World Bank Economic Review* 30, no. 2 (2016): 203–232.

11. The elephant curve is based on data drawn from national household income and expenditure surveys, covering a total of 162 countries across the world at various stages of development.

12. Facundo Alvaredo, Lucas Chancel, Thomas Piketty, Emmanuel Saez, and Gabriel Zucman, eds., *World Inequality Report 2018* (Paris: World Inequality Lab, 2018), 13, https://wir2018.wid.world.

13. The original database on which the updated elephant curve was based included more than a hundred countries across the world spanning all stages of development. The database has been gradually extended; as of 2022, it includes all countries, but the data series is short or incomplete for many countries. See "Methodology," World Inequality Database, accessed October 8, 2022, https://wid.world/methodology.

14. See, for example, Marta Schoch, Christoph Lakner, and Melina Fleury, "Progress toward Ending Poverty Has Slowed," World Bank Data Blog, October 16, 2020, https://blogs.worldbank.org/opendata/progress-toward-ending-poverty-has-slowed.

15. For an empirical study of intranational trade frictions in African countries, see David Atkin and David Donaldson, "Who's Getting Globalized? The Size and Implications of Intra-National Trade Costs" (NBER Working

Paper No. 21439, National Bureau of Economic Research, Cambridge, MA, July 2015), https://www.nber.org/papers/w21439.

16. For an early contribution, see Eli Berman, John Bound, and Zvi Griliches, "Changes in the Demand for Skilled Labor within U.S. Manufacturing: Evidence from the Annual Survey of Manufactures," *Quarterly Journal of Economics* 109, no. 2 (May 1994): 367–397. For an informative overview of the relevant literature, see Adrian Wood, "How Trade Hurt Unskilled Workers," *Journal of Economic Perspectives* 9, no. 3 (Summer 1995): 57–80.

17. See, for example, David Autor and David Dorn, "The Growth of Low-Skill Service Jobs and the Polarization of the U.S. Labor Market," *American Economic Review* 103, no. 5 (August 2013): 1553–1597; David Autor, Lawrence Katz, and Melissa Kearney, "The Polarization of the U.S. Labor Market," *American Economic Review* 96, no. 2 (May 2006): 189–194; Maarten Goos and Alan Manning, "Lousy and Lovely Jobs: The Rising Polarization of Work in Britain," *Review of Economics and Statistics* 89, no. 1 (February 2007): 118–133; Maarten Goos, Alan Manning, and Anna Salomons, "Explaining Job Polarization: Routine-Biased Technological Change and Offshoring," *American Economic Review* 104, no. 8 (August 2014): 2509–2526.

18. It is important to note, however, that the actual pattern of trade and trade protection in several developing countries during this period differed substantially from the one predicted by standard trade models like Heckscher-Ohlin. See Pinelopi Goldberg and Nina Pavcnik, "Trade, Wages, and the Political Economy of Trade Protection: Evidence from the Colombian Trade Reforms," *Journal of International Economics* 66, no. 1 (May 2005): 75–105; Pinelopi Goldberg and Nina Pavcnik, "Distributional Effects of Globalization in Developing Countries," *Journal of Economic Literature* 45, no. 1 (March 2007): 39–82. In Colombia, for example, tariff protection was concentrated on low-skill intensive sectors like textiles and footwear, such that trade liberalization in the 1980s—which reduced tariff protection of such sectors—could not have been expected to benefit low-skill workers. Along the same lines, a recent paper by Rodrigo Adão and colleagues emphasizes that workers are affected by trade through both an export and import channel. Using administrative records from Ecuador, they show that the export channel benefits low-income individuals relative to high-income individuals, while the import channel does the opposite. In the aggregate, they find that the import channel dominates, so that the overall impact of trade is prorich. See Rodrigo Adão, Paul Carrillo, Arnaud Costinot, Dave Donaldson, and Dina Pomeranz, "International Trade and Earnings Inequality: A New Factor Content Approach" (NBER Working Paper No. 28263, National

Bureau of Economic Research, Cambridge, MA, December 2020), https://
www.nber.org/papers/w28263. These studies suggest that the relationship between trade and inequality is nuanced, depending on the import
and export exposure of individuals and firms in specific countries. Hence
the observation that inequality increased in many developing countries in
the 1980s and 1990s—while these countries also significantly liberalized
their foreign trade—does not preclude a trade-based explanation for this
observation. Nevertheless, in quantitative terms, the increase in inequality that one can plausibly attribute to the trade channel is still relatively
small compared to other factors such as technology. For a detailed discussion, see Goldberg and Pavcnik, "Distributional Effects of Globalization
in Developing Countries."

19. Justin Pierce and Peter Schott, "The Surprisingly Swift Decline of US
Manufacturing Employment," *American Economic Review* 106, no. 7 (July
2016): 1632–1662.

20. David Autor, David Dorn, and Gordon Hanson, "The China Syndrome: Local Labor Market Effects of Import Competition in the United
States," *American Economic Review* 103, no. 6 (October 2013): 2121–2168.

21. David Dorn and Peter Levell, "Trade and Inequality in Europe and
the United States," IFS Deaton Review of Inequalities, Institute for Fiscal
Studies, accessed February 28, 2022, https://ifs.org.uk/inequality/trade
-and-inequality-in-europe-and-the-us.

22. Choi, Kuziemko, Washington, and Wright, "Local Employment and
Political Effects of Trade Deals."

23. Goldberg and Pavcnik, "Distributional Effects of Globalization in
Developing Countries." For my earlier work with Pavcnik, see Pinelopi
Goldberg and Nina Pavcnik, "The Response of the Informal Sector to
Trade Liberalization," *Journal of Development Economics* 72, no. 2 (Decem-
ber 2003): 463–496; Pinelopi Goldberg and Nina Pavcnik, "Trade, Inequal-
ity, and Poverty: What Do We Know? Evidence from Recent Trade
Liberalization Episodes in Developing Countries" (NBER Working Paper
No. 10593, National Bureau of Economic Research, Cambridge, MA, June
2004), https://www.nber.org/papers/w10593; Andreas Blom, Pinelopi
Goldberg, Nina Pavcnik, and Norbert Schady, "Trade Liberalization and
Industry Wage Structure: Evidence from Brazil," *World Bank Economic
Review* 18, no. 3 (2004): 319–344; Orazio Attanasio, Pinelopi Goldberg, and
Nina Pavcnik, "Trade Reforms and Wage Inequality in Colombia," *Journal
of Development Economics* 74, no. 2 (August 2004): 331–366; Goldberg and
Pavcnik, "Trade, Wages, and the Political Economy of Trade Protection";
Pinelopi Goldberg and Nina Pavcnik, "The Effects of the Columbian

Trade Liberalization on Urban Poverty," in *Globalization and Poverty*, ed. Ann Harrison (Chicago: University of Chicago Press, 2006), 241–290.

24. Petia Topalova, "Factor Immobility and Regional Impacts of Trade Liberalization: Evidence on Poverty from India," *American Economic Journal: Applied Economics* 2, no. 4 (October 2010): 1–41.

25. Rafael Dix-Carneiro and Brian Kovak, "Trade Liberalization and Regional Dynamics," *American Economic Review* 107, no. 10 (October 2017): 2908–2946.

26. See, for example, Rafael Dix-Carneiro, Pinelopi Goldberg, Costas Meghir, and Gabriel Ulyssea, "Trade and Informality in the Presence of Labor Market Frictions and Regulations" (NBER Working Paper No. 28391, National Bureau of Economic Research, Cambridge, MA, January 2021), https://www.nber.org/papers/w28391.

27. Eric Edmonds, Petia Topalova, and Nina Pavcnik, "Child Labor and Schooling in a Globalizing World: Some Evidence from Urban India," *Journal of the European Economic Association* 7, no. 2–3 (May 2009): 498–507; Eric Edmonds, Nina Pavcnik, and Petia Topalova, "Trade Adjustment and Human Capital Investments: Evidence from Indian Tariff Reform," *American Economic Journal: Applied Economics* 2, no. 4 (October 2010): 42–75.

28. Rafael Dix-Carneiro, Rodrigo Soares, and Gabriel Ulyssea, "Economic Shocks and Crime: Evidence from the Brazilian Trade Liberalization," *American Economic Journal: Applied Economics* 10, no. 4 (October 2018): 158–195.

29. Jan De Loecker, Pinelopi Goldberg, Amit Khandelwal, and Nina Pavcnik, "Prices, Markups and Trade Reform," *Econometrica* 84, no. 2 (March 2016): 445–510.

30. In the economics literature, this phenomenon of cost reductions not being passed through one for one to prices is known as "incomplete pass-through." The incomplete pass-through of the cost reductions from trade is similar to the "incomplete exchange rate pass-through" that has been well documented in the international macroeconomics literature.

31. Jan De Loecker, Jan Eeckhout, and Gabriel Unger, "The Rise of Market Power and the Macroeconomic Implications," *Quarterly Journal of Economics* 135, no. 2 (May 2020): 561–644.

32. Jan De Loecker and Jan Eeckhout, "Global Market Power" (NBER Working Paper No. 24768, National Bureau of Economic Research, Cambridge, MA, June 2018), https://www.nber.org/papers/w24768.

33. "Backward participation" involves buying part of the supply chain that occurs prior to the company's manufacturing process; in the international context, where parts of the supply chain are located in different countries, one can think of backward integration as "importing to export" (e.g., importing intermediates or semifinished goods in order to manufacture finished products that are then exported to other countries). Many advanced countries engage in this type of backward integration by importing parts or intermediate products from developing countries, where costs are typically lower. In contrast, "forward participation" involves business activities that are ahead in the value chain of a company's industry; in the international context, one can think of forward integration as "exporting to export" (e.g., exporting raw materials or parts and components to a different country, where they are used to manufacture products that are then exported to different countries). Many developing countries are involved in this type of forward integration.

34. World Bank, *World Development Report 2020: Trading for Development in the Age of Global Value Chains* (Washington, DC: World Bank, 2019).

35. David Atkin, Benjamin Faber, and Marco Gonzalez-Navarro, "Retail Globalization and Household Welfare: Evidence from Mexico," *Journal of Political Economy* 126, no. 1 (February 2018): 1–73.

36. Xavier Jaravel and Erick Sager, "What Are the Price Effects of Trade? Evidence from the US and Implications for Quantitative Trade Models" (Centre for Economic Performance Discussion Paper No. 1642, London School of Economics, August 2019), https://cep.lse.ac.uk/pubs/download/dp1642.pdf.

37. Dorn and Levell, "Trade and Inequality in Europe and the United States."

38. Kirill Borusyak and Xavier Jaravel, "The Distributional Effects of Trade: Theory and Evidence from the United States" (NBER Working Paper 28957, National Bureau of Economic Research, Cambridge, MA, June 2021), http://www.nber.org/papers/w28957.

39. Pablo Fajgelbaum and Amit Khandelwal, "Measuring the Unequal Gains from Trade," *Quarterly Journal of Economics* 131, no. 3 (August 2016): 1113–1180.

40. David Atkin, "Trade and Price-Index Inequality," IFS Deaton Review of Inequalities, Institute for Fiscal Studies, accessed February 28, 2022, https://ifs.org.uk/inequality/trade-and-price-index-inequality.

Chapter 3

1. See Pablo Fajgelbaum, Pinelopi Goldberg, Patrick Kennedy, Amit Khandelwal, and Daria Taglioni, "The US-China Trade War and Global Reallocations" (NBER Working Paper No. 29562, National Bureau of Economic Research, Cambridge, MA, December 2021), https://www.nber.org/papers/w29562.

2. Pol Antras, "De-Globalisation? Global Value Chains in the Post-COVID-19 Age," ECB Forum on Central Banking, European Central Bank, November 2020.

Bibliography

Adão, Rodrigo, Paul Carrillo, Arnaud Costinot, Dave Donaldson, and Dina Pomeranz. "International Trade and Earnings Inequality: A New Factor Content Approach." NBER Working Paper No. 28263, National Bureau of Economic Research, Cambridge, MA, December 2020. https://www.nber.org/papers/w28263.

Altman, Roger C., and Richard N. Haass. "Why the Trans-Pacific Partnership Matters." *New York Times*, April 3, 2015. https://www.nytimes.com/2015/04/04/opinion/why-the-trans-pacific-partnership-matters.html.

Alvaredo, Facundo, Lucas Chancel, Thomas Piketty, Emmanuel Saez, and Gabriel Zucman, eds. *World Inequality Report 2018*. Paris: World Inequality Lab, 2018. https://wir2018.wid.world.

Antras, Pol. "De-Globalisation? Global Value Chains in the Post-COVID-19 Age." ECB Forum on Central Banking, European Central Bank, November 2020.

Arkolakis, Costas, Arnaud Costinot, and Andres Rodríguez-Clare. "New Trade Models, Same Old Gains?" *American Economic Review* 102, no. 1 (February 2012): 94–130.

Atkin, David. "Trade and Price-Index Inequality." IFS Deaton Review of Inequalities, Institute for Fiscal Studies. Accessed February 28, 2022. https://ifs.org.uk/inequality/trade-and-price-index-inequality.

Atkin, David, and David Donaldson. "Who's Getting Globalized? The Size and Implications of Intra-National Trade Costs." NBER Working Paper No. 21439, National Bureau of Economic Research, Cambridge, MA, July 2015. https://www.nber.org/papers/w21439.

Atkin, David, Benjamin Faber, and Marco Gonzalez-Navarro. "Retail Globalization and Household Welfare: Evidence from Mexico." *Journal of Political Economy* 126, no. 1 (February 2018): 1–73.

Attanasio, Orazio, Pinelopi Goldberg, and Nina Pavcnik. "Trade Reforms and Wage Inequality in Colombia." *Journal of Development Economics* 74, no. 2 (August 2004): 331–366.

Autor, David, and David Dorn. "The Growth of Low-Skill Service Jobs and the Polarization of the U.S. Labor Market." *American Economic Review* 103, no. 5 (August 2013): 1553–1597.

Autor, David, David Dorn, and Gordon Hanson. "The China Syndrome: Local Labor Market Effects of Import Competition in the United States." *American Economic Review* 103, no. 6 (October 2013): 2121–2168.

Autor, David, David Dorn, Gordon Hanson, and Kaveh Majlesi. "Importing Political Polarization? The Electoral Consequences of Rising Trade Exposure." *American Economic Review* 110, no. 10 (October 2020): 3139–3183.

Autor, David, Lawrence Katz, and Melissa Kearney. "The Polarization of the U.S. Labor Market." *American Economic Review* 96, no. 2 (May 2006): 189–194.

Baldwin, Richard. "Global Supply Chains: Why They Emerged, Why They Matter, and Where They Are Going." CEPR Discussion Paper 9103, Centre for Economic Policy Research, August 2012. https://cepr.org /active/publications/discussion_papers/dp.php?dpno=9103.

Berman, Eli, John Bound, and Zvi Griliches. "Changes in the Demand for Skilled Labor within U.S. Manufacturing: Evidence from the Annual Survey of Manufactures." *Quarterly Journal of Economics* 109, no. 2 (May 1994): 367–397.

Blom, Andreas, Pinelopi Goldberg, Nina Pavcnik, and Norbert Schady. "Trade Liberalization and Industry Wage Structure: Evidence from Brazil." *World Bank Economic Review* 18, no. 3 (2004): 319–344.

Borin, Alessandro, and Michele Mancini. "Follow the Value Added: Bilateral Gross Export Accounting." Temi di discussione (Economic Working Paper) 1026, Economic Research and International Relations Area, Bank of Italy, 2015.

Borin, Alessandro, and Michele Mancini. "Measuring What Matters in Global Value Chains and Value-Added Trade." Policy Research Working Paper 8804, World Bank, Washington, DC, April 2019. https://open knowledge.worldbank.org/handle/10986/31533.

Borusyak, Kirill, and Xavier Jaravel. "The Distributional Effects of Trade: Theory and Evidence from the United States." NBER Working Paper

28957, National Bureau of Economic Research, Cambridge, MA, June 2021. http://www.nber.org/papers/w28957.

Chaudhuri, Shubham, Pinelopi Goldberg, and Panle Jia. "Estimating the Effects of Global Patent Protection in Pharmaceuticals: A Case Study of Quinolones in India." *American Economic Review* 96, no. 5 (December 2006): 1477–1514.

Che, Yi, Yi Lu, Justin Pierce, Peter Schott, and Zhigang Tao. "Does Trade Liberalization with China Influence US Elections?" NBER Working Paper No. 22178, National Bureau of Economic Research, Cambridge, MA, April 2016. https://www.nber.org/papers/w22178.

Choi, Jiwon, Ilyana Kuziemko, Ebonya Washington, and Gavin Wright. "Local Employment and Political Effects of Trade Deals: Evidence from NAFTA." NBER Working Paper No. 29525, National Bureau of Economic Research, Cambridge, MA, November 2021. https://www.nber.org/papers/w29525.

Clemens, Michael, and Jeffrey Williamson. "Why Did the Tariff-Growth Correlation Change after 1950?" *Journal of Economic Growth* 9, no. 1 (March 2004): 5–46.

Colantone, Italo, and Piero Stanig. "Global Competition and Brexit." *American Political Science Review* 112, no. 2 (May 2018): 201–218.

Deardorff, Alan, and Robert Stern. *The Michigan Model of World Production and Trade: Theory and Applications.* Cambridge, MA: MIT Press, 1985.

Deaton, Angus. *The Great Escape: Health, Wealth, and the Origins of Inequality.* Princeton, NJ: Princeton University Press, 2013.

De Loecker, Jan, and Jan Eeckhout. "Global Market Power." NBER Working Paper No. 24768, National Bureau of Economic Research, Cambridge, MA, June 2018. https://www.nber.org/papers/w24768.

De Loecker, Jan, Jan Eeckhout, and Gabriel Unger. "The Rise of Market Power and the Macroeconomic Implications." *Quarterly Journal of Economics* 135, no. 2 (May 2020): 561–644.

De Loecker, Jan, Pinelopi Goldberg, Amit Khandelwal, and Nina Pavcnik. "Prices, Markups and Trade Reform." *Econometrica* 84, no. 2 (March 2016): 445–510.

Dippel, Christian, Robert Gold, and Stephan Heblich. "Globalization and Its (Dis-)Content: Trade Shocks and Voting Behavior." NBER Working Paper No. 21812, National Bureau of Economic Research, Cambridge, MA, December 2015. https://www.nber.org/papers/w21812.

Dix-Carneiro, Rafael, Pinelopi Goldberg, Costas Meghir, and Gabriel Ulyssea. "Trade and Informality in the Presence of Labor Market Frictions and Regulations." NBER Working Paper No. 28391, National Bureau of Economic Research, Cambridge, MA, January 2021. https://www.nber.org/papers/w28391.

Dix-Carneiro, Rafael, and Brian Kovak. "Trade Liberalization and Regional Dynamics." *American Economic Review* 107, no. 10 (October 2017): 2908–2946.

Dix-Carneiro, Rafael, Rodrigo Soares, and Gabriel Ulyssea. "Economic Shocks and Crime: Evidence from the Brazilian Trade Liberalization." *American Economic Journal: Applied Economics* 10, no. 4 (October 2018): 158–195.

Dorn, David, and Peter Levell. "Trade and Inequality in Europe and the United States." IFS Deaton Review, Institute for Fiscal Studies. Accessed February 28, 2022. https://ifs.org.uk/inequality/trade-and-inequality-in-europe-and-the-us.

Edmonds, Eric, Nina Pavcnik, and Petia Topalova. "Trade Adjustment and Human Capital Investments: Evidence from Indian Tariff Reform." *American Economic Journal: Applied Economics* 2, no. 4 (October 2010): 42–75.

Edmonds, Eric, Petia Topalova, and Nina Pavcnik. "Child Labor and Schooling in a Globalizing World: Some Evidence from Urban India." *Journal of the European Economic Association* 7, no. 2–3 (May 2009): 498–507.

Fajgelbaum, Pablo, Pinelopi Goldberg, Patrick Kennedy, and Amit Khandelwal. "The Return to Protectionism." *Quarterly Journal of Economics* 135, no. 1 (February 2020): 1–55.

Fajgelbaum, Pablo, Pinelopi Goldberg, Patrick Kennedy, Amit Khandelwal, and Daria Taglioni. "The US-China Trade War and Global Reallocations." NBER Working Paper No. 29562, National Bureau of Economic Research, Cambridge, MA, December 2021. https://www.nber.org/papers/w29562.

Fajgelbaum, Pablo, and Amit Khandelwal. "Measuring the Unequal Gains from Trade." *Quarterly Journal of Economics* 131, no. 3 (August 2016): 1113–1180.

Fouquin, Michel, and Jules Hugot. "Two Centuries of Bilateral Trade and Gravity Data: 1827–2014." CEPII Working Paper No. 2016–14, May 2016. http://www.cepii.fr/pdf_pub/wp/2016/wp2016-14.pdf.

Goldberg, Pinelopi. "The Future of Trade." IMF Finance and Development, June 2019. https://www.elibrary.imf.org/view/journals/022/2019/002/022.2019.issue-002-en.xml.

Goldberg, Pinelopi. "Intellectual Property Rights Protection in Developing Countries: The Case of Pharmaceuticals." *Journal of the European Economic Association* 8, no. 2–3 (May 2010): 326–353.

Goldberg, Pinelopi, and Nina Pavcnik. "Distributional Effects of Globalization in Developing Countries." *Journal of Economic Literature* 45, no. 1 (March 2007): 39–82.

Goldberg, Pinelopi, and Nina Pavcnik. "The Effects of the Columbian Trade Liberalization on Urban Poverty." In *Globalization and Poverty*, edited by Ann Harrison, 241–290. Chicago: University of Chicago Press, 2006.

Goldberg, Pinelopi, and Nina Pavcnik. "The Effects of Trade Policy." In *Handbook of Commercial Policy (Volume 1, Part A)*, edited by Kyle Bagwell and Robert Staiger, 161–206. Amsterdam: Elsevier, 2016.

Goldberg, Pinelopi, and Nina Pavcnik. "The Response of the Informal Sector to Trade Liberalization." *Journal of Development Economics*, 72, no. 2 (December 2003): 463–496.

Goldberg, Pinelopi, and Nina Pavcnik. "Trade, Inequality, and Poverty: What Do We Know? Evidence from Recent Trade Liberalization Episodes in Developing Countries." NBER Working Paper No. 10593, National Bureau of Economic Research, Cambridge, MA, June 2004. https://www.nber.org/papers/w10593.

Goldberg, Pinelopi, and Nina Pavcnik. "Trade, Wages, and the Political Economy of Trade Protection: Evidence from the Colombian Trade Reforms." *Journal of International Economics* 66, no. 1 (May 2005): 75–105.

Goldberg, Pinelopi, and Tristan Reed. "Income Distribution, International Integration and Sustained Poverty Reduction." Policy Research Working Paper No. 9342, World Bank, Washington, DC, July 2020. https://openknowledge.worldbank.org/handle/10986/34260.

Goos, Maarten, and Alan Manning. "Lousy and Lovely Jobs: The Rising Polarization of Work in Britain." *Review of Economics and Statistics* 89, no. 1 (February 2007): 118–133.

Goos, Maarten, Alan Manning, and Anna Salomons. "Explaining Job Polarization: Routine-Biased Technological Change and Offshoring." *American Economic Review* 104, no. 8 (August 2014): 2509–2526.

Hofmann, Claudia, Alberto Osnago, and Michele Ruta. "Horizontal Depth: A New Database on the Content of Preferential Trade Agreements." Policy Research Working Paper No. 7981, World Bank, Washington, DC, February 2017. https://openknowledge.worldbank.org/handle/10986/26148.

IFS Deaton Review. Institute for Fiscal Studies. Accessed February 28, 2022. https://ifs.org.uk/inequality.

Jaravel, Xavier, and Erick Sager. "What Are the Price Effects of Trade? Evidence from the US and Implications for Quantitative Trade Models." Centre for Economic Performance Discussion Paper No. 1642, London School of Economics, August 2019. https://cep.lse.ac.uk/pubs/download/dp1642.pdf.

Johnson, Robert, and Guillermo Noguera. "A Portrait of Trade in Value Added over Four Decades." *Review of Economics and Statistics* 99, no. 5 (December 2017): 896–911.

Kinzius, Luisa, Alexander Sandkamp, and Erdal Yalcin. "Trade Protection and the Role of Non-Tariff Barriers." *Review of World Economics* 155, no. 4 (November 2019): 603–643.

Krugman, Paul. "Growing World Trade: Causes and Consequences." *Brookings Papers on Economic Activity* 1 (1995): 327–377.

Lakner, Christoph, and Branko Milanovic. "Global Income Distribution: From the Fall of the Berlin Wall to the Great Recession." *World Bank Economic Review* 30, no. 2 (2016): 203–232.

Malgouyres, Clément. "Trade Shocks and Far-Right Voting: Evidence from French Presidential Elections." Robert Schuman Centre for Advanced Studies Research Paper No. RSCAS 2017/21, Florence, Italy, March 2017.

Mayda, Anna Maria, and Dani Rodrik. "Why Are Some People (and Countries) More Protectionist than Others?" *European Economic Review* 49, no. 6 (August 2005): 1393–1430.

Méndez-Chacón, Esteban, and Diana van Patten. "Voting on a Trade Agreement: Firm Networks and Attitudes toward Openness." NBER Working Paper No. 30058, National Bureau of Economic Research, Cambridge, MA, May 2022. https://www.nber.org/papers/w30058.

Milanovic, Branko. *Global Inequality: A New Approach for the Age of Globalization.* Cambridge, MA: Harvard University Press, 2016.

Pavcnik, Nina. "The Impact of Trade on Inequality in Developing Countries." *Jackson Hole Economic Policy Symposium Proceedings*, 61–114. Kansas City: Federal Reserve Bank of Kansas City, August 2017.

Pierce, Justin, and Peter Schott. "The Surprisingly Swift Decline of US Manufacturing Employment." *American Economic Review* 106, no. 7 (July 2016): 1632–1662.

Pritchett, Lant. "Immigration: Ending Global Apartheid." Interview by Kerry Howley. *Reason*, February 2008. https://reason.com/2008/01/24/ending-global-apartheid.

Rodrigue, Jean-Paul, Claude Comtois, and Brian Slack. *The Geography of Transport Systems*, 4th ed. New York: Routledge, 2017.

Rose, Andrew. "Do We Really Know That the WTO Increases Trade?" *American Economic Review* 94, no. 1 (March 2004): 98–114.

Schoch, Marta, Christoph Lakner, and Melina Fleury. "Progress toward Ending Poverty Has Slowed." World Bank Data Blog, October 16, 2020. https://blogs.worldbank.org/opendata/progress-toward-ending-poverty-has-slowed.

Topalova, Petia. "Factor Immobility and Regional Impacts of Trade Liberalization: Evidence on Poverty from India." *American Economic Journal: Applied Economics* 2, no. 4 (October 2010): 1–41.

Wood, Adrian. "How Trade Hurt Unskilled Workers." *Journal of Economic Perspectives* 9, no. 3 (Summer 1995): 57–80.

World Bank. "Exports of Goods and Services (% of GDP)." World Bank Group. Accessed July 25, 2022. https://data.worldbank.org/indicator/NE.EXP.GNFS.ZS.

World Bank. *World Development Report 2006: Equity and Development.* Washington, DC: World Bank, 2006.

World Bank. *World Development Report 2020: Trading for Development in the Age of Global Value Chains.* Washington, DC: World Bank, 2019.

Yi, Kei-Mu. "Can Vertical Specialization Explain the Growth of World Trade?" *Journal of Political Economy* 111, no. 1 (February 2003): 52–102.

Yonzan, Nishant, Christoph Lakner, and Daniel Gerszon Mahler. "Projecting Global Extreme Poverty up to 2030: How Close Are We to World Bank's 3% Goal?" World Bank Data Blog, October 9, 2020. https://blogs.worldbank.org/opendata/projecting-global-extreme-poverty-2030-how-close-are-we-world-banks-3-goal.

Index